God's KINGDOM CULTURE

WILLIAM A. DOCKERY

To my wife, Pearlie,
who has been my encouragement to complete
the assignment I have been given by the Lord.
Your love, loyalty, faith, and wisdom
have been my strength.

To my Daughter Andrea, her husband George,
and my son William Shawn as they continue to
serve faithfully in the Kingdom of God.

To Memorial Temple Christian Ministries &
Covenant Ministries International.

To those who hunger and thirst after
the righteousness of God. May this book serve
to make your journey more fruitful!

To the Believers in Christ committed to the
removal of cultural and denominational barriers
for the purpose of kingdom expansion and
the unity of the Saints.

*...that it might be fulfilled which was spoken
by the prophet, saying: "I will open My mouth in
parables; I will utter things kept secret from
the foundation of the world.*
Psalms 78:2, quoted in Matthew 13:35

*I have not written to you because
you do not know the truth, but because you
know it, and that no lie is of the truth.*
1 John 2:21

What is this awesome mystery
That is taking place within me?
I can find no words to express it;
my poor hand is unable to capture it
In describing the praise and glory that belong
to the One who is above all praise,
and who transcends every word...
but it cannot explain it.
It can see, and wishes to explain,
but can find no word that will suffice:
For what it sees is invisible and entirely formless,
simple, completely uncompounded,
unbounded in its awesome greatness.
What I have seen is the totality recapitulated as one,
received not in essence but by participation.
Just as if you lit a flame from a flame,
It is the whole flame you receive.

ST. SYMEON THE NEW THEOLOGIAN (949-1022)

CONTENTS

———

INTRODUCTION   *xi*

God's Kingdom Culture   1
Being Used by God   18
One God   33
The Power of Criticism   49
Our Identity in Christ   63
The School of Love   77

SCRIPTURE INDEX   *95*
RESOURCES   *99*
ABOUT THE AUTHOR   *101*

INTRODUCTION

—

This book is based on various subjects in Scripture that are vital in aiding Christians in their ability to navigate through the darkness of trials and adversity. This will help the believer to obtain growth and maturity in our Lord and Savior Jesus Christ. Of course, the Word of God is filled with wisdom on how to get it right and how to get it wrong. The genius of biblical revelation is that it just doesn't give us the conclusions; it gives us the process of getting there. It also shows us that our destiny is not a straight line, but a three steps forward and two steps backward motion. Yet the believer, who walks by faith, knows their destiny is sure because of the work the Lord has started in us.

In this life we cannot reach that place in God where there is contentment, peace, and oneness through our intellect regardless of our educational status; or through our imagination, or through our senses. It is only through faith in the Word of God, hope in the exceedingly great and precious promises of God, and the love that flows from God through His Son to us. It is through the blending of these three virtues that make up the foundation, enabling one to journey to a place whereby we are able to finally impact the lives of others.

Jesus said, "You must be born again in order to enter the Kingdom of Heaven." By this he meant that you had to be born once to the world, and once again to the knowledge of God through Him. I have come to believe that we now must be born three times. Once to the world, once to God, and once to ourselves. Because only when we can see who we are and what we stand for, what we want to be about in the world; only then does every action we take suddenly seem significant. That is the point at which we have realized a vision of ourselves and our path through this world. It is a path that defines our own true destiny.

Today's Events in Summary

We are now living in a time of a deadly global pandemic called Covid-19, also known as the coronavirus. A virus that has now killed in America alone over 400,000 people in approximately eleven months, and is continuing to take lives even as a vaccine is now being administered. Again, this virus is not just in America but has spread all over the world, effecting millions and destroying economies.

We in America have a deeply divided government that seems to have no common ground to come together for solutions to the massive problems facing our society. Strange weather patterns producing unusual storms and floods. There is drought in the west—fires destroying homes amid acres and acres of forestry. In the midst of this, great exposure has come to systemic racism in America as a result of social media, cellphone cameras capturing police brutality. Excessive force used in cases of arresting and restraining Black and Brown people, even to the point of death. Protesting and rioting has become the standard activity in many American cities because there is a refusal to acknowledge the ongoing injustice in the top echelon of our government.

Unemployment is at an all-time high and still increasing. If I were to write in detail of the ever increasing problems facing the United States, I would need to write another book just to touch on the depth of the issues relating to the political, social, economic, and climate issues facing this nation currently. Not to mention the fact that we have just concluded the most critical election of our times.

I am reminded of the words of Thomas Paine who on December 19, 1776 publish a journal entitled "The American Crisis." He writes, "These are the times that try men's souls; the summer soldier and the sunshine patriot will in this crisis, shrink from the service of his country; but he that stands it now, deserves the love and thanks of man and woman." He went on to say, "Tyranny, like hell, is not easily conquered; yet we have this consolation with us, that the harder the conflict, the more glorious the triumph." These words inspired General Washington's troops, as this journal was read to them as they were overcome by the renowned British General Earl Cornwallis. They mustered the strength and courage to finally win the American Revolution.

I believe that in this hour of great trial and crisis, there is a reconfiguration of the People of God and the Church of the Lord Jesus Christ taking place. Not just because of Covid-19, but the culmination of everything that is occurring. Due to Covid-19 in particular there has been a great change in the way church is done. Many ministries are forced to meet on Zoom or other kinds of social media to protect their congregations. There are those who have purchased tents for outdoor meetings as weather permits. Mass crowds are forbidden for fear of spreading the virus even more. Many of those who have been in defiance to basic rules, such as the wearing of a mask, washing hands, and staying out of large crowds, have become prey to the virus and have lost their lives. Great numbers of pastors, bishops, spiritual leaders, and congregants have succumb to the disease; some as it were, in defiance to general rules, and some just as a result of the changing of the guard in leadership. There is a reckoning we must all come to grips with, and that is whether church is a hobby, or whether it is a matter of conscience and faith.

I say to you that there are a people who have taken hold of the horns of the altar. They are not known by any political persuasion or denominational tag; they are not known for any particular cause or affiliate; they are a people after the heart of the Father—intercessors who are crying out to the Lord, day and night with fasting saying, "thy Kingdom Come, thy will be done on earth as it is in heaven." This cry is ushering in an end time revival, a move of God, the likes of which we have never seen before. There is a new wineskin being developed that will be a container for the new wine of the Spirit being poured out in this hour. This will cause the Church and the people of God to rise above the ashes of crisis, despair, and hopelessness, like a phoenix. There is a harvest of souls that will be accomplished and the Glory of the Lord shall be revealed..... Amen!

ONE

God's Kingdom Culture

And from Jesus Christ the faithful and trustworthy
Witness, the Firstborn of the dead [first to be brought
back to life] and the Prince (Ruler) of the kings of the
earth. To Him Who ever loves us and has once [for all]
loosed and freed us from our sins by His own blood,
And formed us into a kingdom (a royal race), priests to
His God and Father—to Him be the glory and the power
and the majesty and the dominion throughout the ages
and forever and ever. Amen (so be it).
REVELATIONS 1:5-6 (AMP)

That He might present the church to Himself in glori-
ous splendor, without spot or wrinkle or any such things
[that she might be holy and faultless].
EPHESIANS 5:27 (AMP)

The Word "culture" derives from a French term, which in turn derives from the Latin *colere,* which means to tend to the earth and grow, or cultivation and nurture. When we talk about culture we are referring to belief

systems, values, and behaviors that support a particular ideology or social arrangement. It's a word for the way of life of
people, meaning the way they do things.

As far as the church is concerned, the largest and most
widespread barrier that we have any control over that keeps
people from faith is the culture barrier. I might also inject the
fact that "the strongest force in an organization is not vision
or strategy—it is the culture which holds all the other components," says Sam Chand, author of *Cracking Your Church's
Culture*. Every leader at some time or the other has asked the
same question: "Why is it that we are not where I know we
should be as a church?"

If there is anything one can discern, it is culture, whether it
is a restaurant, school, clothing store, grocery store or church,
or even someone's home. There is a climate that either inspires
you to return or inspires you not to return. In my own experience in dealing with the unchurched, most already have a pre-
conceived notion about church culture in general they reject.
Many people resist the church because they don't want to
lose their identity and become like church people, which they
believe is a prerequisite for becoming a Christian.

Something in the church's "body language" shouts more
loudly than the new life and the new lifestyle embodied in
some of the members. Unchurched people are struck first,
and put off, by the dated or alien church subculture. And in
many ways it is a distant subculture with its own values, cus-
toms, norms, habits, language, music, aesthetics, etc.

I must say that it is not all the church's issues that keep the
seeker from the church. Some barriers are within the heart of
the seeker. Some love their sins more than they want to love
God. Some want their agenda more than God's agenda. The
souls of some people are not quite ready for now because of

being fixed to some idol, and their hearts are hardened and not open to the gospel's message.

For the most part when unchurched people talk about "church people," unfortunately they do not refer to people who transparently love God and their neighbors, who serve the community and live for others. People who come from a background of manipulation and insincerity will not be influenced to Christ by superficial halfhearted witnessing. 1 John says; "If we love one another, God abides in us, and His love has been perfected in us" (4:12). Our job is to faithfully love the people God has given us to love, whether there are two or two hundred of them. If God sees we are ready to love others, He will bring them to us. Regardless of our personality, God have given us the power to be effective in our witness to bring people to Christ. Paul says, "So then neither he who plants is anything, nor he who waters, but God who gives the increase" (1 Cor. 3:7). We need to be conscious of the fact that we are workers together with God.

One of the greatest issues we are contending with is reaching people in our own culture. We must be able to develop a lifestyle of reaching out to people who are just like us. If we can't bring our own culture in, we will probably never be able to reach out to people who are different from us. Crossing cultural barriers adds a whole new dimension to seeking the unchurched. If reaching people in our own culture and language is difficult for most of us, reaching those of another culture will be even more so. As individuals and churches— we need to first develop the habit of caring about, loving, and sharing the Gospel with those that are like us. Once this becomes a natural part of our lives, we can build on this experience, taking it to the next level of reaching those of a different culture or background.

Bridge Building

Now then, we are ambassadors for Christ, as though God were pleading through us: we implore *you* on Christ's behalf, be reconciled to God. For He made Him who knew no sin *to be* sin for us, that we might become the righteousness of God in Him. (2 Corinthians 5:20-21)

Paul was writing to the Church of Corinth with a burning awareness of the apostolic calling of that church even as he himself was called. As Paul himself was commissioned to serve as an envoy in a foreign—even hostile—land, so it is with individuals and the church today. As ambassadors for Christ, we have the responsibility of representing His sovereign or government, whose cause we are proud to plead because the Lord has equipped us with power from on high to do so.

As ambassadors of Christ or ministers of the Word of God, we are actually crossing cultural barriers. We are building a bridge by means of communication between two places which would otherwise be cut off from one another by a river, ravine, or some chasm or gulf. This bridge of communication makes possible a flow of traffic, without which it would be impossible. What, then, does the gorge or chasm represent? And what is the bridge which spans it? The chasm is the deep rift between the biblical world and the modern world. It is across this broad and deep divide of some two thousand years of changing culture, and even more considering the Old Testament, that Christian communicators have to throw bridges. Our task is to enable God's revealed truth to flow out of the Scriptures into the lives of the people today.

For many people today, even Christians, the issue of

contention is not so much the truth of the Word, it is the relevance of the Word of God. For example: How do we make the Word of God applicable to our lives today, bridging the cultural gap from ancient times to today's lifestyle? Certainly, we must plunge fearlessly into both worlds, ancient and modern, biblical and contemporary, and listen attentively to both. For only then shall we understand what each is saying, and so discern the Spirit's message to this present generation. We have to ask says John Scott, author of *Between Two Worlds*, in the controversial language of Dietrich Bonhoeffer, "Who is Christ for us today?" Already in 1932 he said, "The point is not how we are to model the message, but what really is the message and its content for the present age?"

The task of building bridges must be the passion of the believer in cross-cultural relationships as well. Integration is intentional, and passionate; it can't be done through passivity or a casual attitude. People know when they are being treated as a project of some kind to appease the ego of an individual, as opposed to being treated with real, genuine, and authentic love. Jesus was always moved with compassion as he looked upon the needs of the people. This is what enabled him to receive from the Father all that was needed for the people—whether it was healing, raising the dead, or feeding the multitudes with the fish and the loaves of bread.

Church History

Even in church history, the church has seemed to require people to "become like us" culturally for a very long time. We find this pattern as early as the history recorded in Acts 15. The early church in Jerusalem was requiring their Gentile converts to become circumcised, give up pork, obey Sabbath laws and their rules and regulations, and become culturally Jewish as a requirement for becoming baptized followers of Jesus the Messiah. Meanwhile, up in Antioch, Gentiles were becoming disciples in great numbers but were not also practicing Jewish Laws. This created a crisis at "The Jerusalem Council" that is reported in Acts 15. After the parties of James, Paul, and Simon Peter deliberated the issue, the council determined that Gentiles did not have to become culturally kosher to follow Christ and be part of his movement.

The Jerusalem Council's decision was momentous. Without that decision, Christianity might have remained a sect of "fulfilled Jews" within Judaism. The decision extended the principle of Incarnation; as Jesus had adapted to Galilean Aramaic-speaking peasant culture, so the church, his Body, could now become "indigenous" to all the cultures of the earth. Now that Gentiles did not have to become Jews to become Christians, the faith was unleashed to spread and adapt within three centuries to most of the major cultures in the Roman Empire, and to later become the world's most universal faith.

It would seem that the Jerusalem Council settled a very significant matter, and it did. But Christianity has struggled with the problem, in many versions, ever since. In the years following the Jerusalem council, the party of James (the "Judaizers") reverted to Plan A, and decided that Jewish enculturation was a necessary part of Christian discipleship after all. The Judaizers even grew for a while, and they fanned out across the Mediterranean world—stirring up people in several churches Paul had planted, prompting several letters from Paul, notably his Letter to the Galatians.

In one way, at least, the party of Paul failed to fully implement the Jerusalem Council's decision. The Christian movement became predominantly Gentile, and throughout most of our history Jewish people have not become Christians, in part because they felt required to become culturally Gentile as a prerequisite to becoming Christian! Only in the last quarter century has the church enabled a Jewish Christian movement, employing the cultural forms of Jews to reach and nurture Jews. Consequently, through Jews For Jesus and the Messianic Synagogue movement, an unprecedented number of Jews have become fulfilled Jews.

The Culture Barrier Today

Martin Robinson's book, *A World Apart*, observes that the Church's "cultural blindness" prevents it from even perceiving "the distinction between the gospel and the cultural forms in which we express it," and that fact, "is responsible for a great deal of the failure of the church to make a significant impact on the society of which we are a part."

The culture barrier is an even bigger problem for mainline American Christianity, because we bought the early twentieth century myth of the "American Melting Pot." That myth taught that people come from the nations of the other continents and enter a "melting pot" experience in which everyone comes out as assimilated mainline Americans. But the myth really assumed a more imperialistic process—that people who come from the earth's various nations should become like those of us whose ancestors came from Great Britain! So American Christianity has added to the usual expectations that the people who join our churches and those with whom we fellowship will become "like us, or already be like us." But with the rise of what Michael Novak called "the unmeltable ethnics," we observe people of many cultures and subcultures whose culture seems as natural to them as ours does to us, who like their art, music, style, and language or dialect about as much as we like ours, who are not motivated to "become circumcised" and become like us.

A salad bowl or tossed salad is a metaphor for the way a multicultural society can integrate different cultures while maintaining their separate identities, contrasting with a melting pot, which emphasizes the combination of the parts into a single whole.

The Lord wants a healthy church in all of its diversity. Ephesians 5 lets us know that he both gives and takes the bride; he presents her to himself—the day of his espousals being in the state of glory. John testified, "And I John saw the holy city, new Jerusalem, coming down from God out of heaven, prepared as a bride adorned for her husband" (Rev 21:2). And all the training of this life being designed to fit her for that condition, she becomes glorious at last through assimilation to himself. John says, "And the glory which thou gave me I have given them; that they may be one, even as we are one" (John 17:22).

God's Kingdom

There is a distinction between the Church and the Kingdom of God. The definition of the word "kingdom" in Greek is *basileia*—or "a king's domain; the fact of being king by his power and position." The status of the king is shown by the area over which he reigns, or governs as having total control. It also indicates the rule of the king in the lives of willing subjects. There is a culture that is fixed by God, it does not change according to the time or season or people. Our Lord has set the culture, the order from the beginning of time.

When we speak of the Kingdom of God, we are speaking of the rule and government of the Lord Jesus Christ upon your life; this is evidenced by a continual obedience to the spiritual laws of this kingdom. The Kingdom message is "Repent for the Kingdom of Heaven is at hand." This was preached first by John the Baptist, then Jesus, then by Jesus's disciples (Matthew 3:2 / 4:17 / 10:7). In the book of Acts, Luke writes concerning Jesus after his resurrection; "....being seen by them during forty days and speaking of the things pertaining to the kingdom of God." (1:3) Again in the book of Matthew, Jesus says, "And this gospel of the kingdom will be preached in all the world as a witness to all the nations, and then the end will come." (24:14).

The idea of the Kingdom of God is expressed by the Psalmist when he says; "All Your works shall praise You, O LORD, And Your saints shall bless You. They shall speak of the glory of Your kingdom, And talk of Your power, To make known to the sons of men His mighty acts, And the glorious majesty of His kingdom. Your kingdom *is* an everlasting kingdom, And Your dominion *endures* throughout all generations." (Psalm 145:10-12)

We see also that "the kingdom of God *is* not in word but in power." (1 Cor. 4:20) Again Apostle Paul says, "for the kingdom of God is not eating and drinking, but righteousness and peace and joy in the Holy Spirit" (Romans 14:17). Hebrews tells us; "Therefore, since we are receiving a kingdom which cannot be shaken, let us have grace, by which we may serve God acceptably with reverence and godly fear. For our God *is* a consuming fire." (12:28-29) All of these Scriptures gives us insight into the nature, concept, and idea of the Kingdom of God.

We enter the Kingdom of God by embracing the Lord Jesus Christ. This is made remarkably clear through the following Scriptures. "And she will bring forth a Son, and you shall call His name JESUS, for He will save His people from their sins" (Matthew 1:21). In Matthew "Simon Peter answered and said, 'You are the Christ, the Son of the living God.'...Then He commanded His disciples that they should tell no one that He was Jesus the Christ" (16:16 / 20). The Apostle Paul spoke specifically to entering the Kingdom of God in Romans, stating, "that if you confess with your mouth the Lord Jesus and believe in your heart that God has raised Him from the dead, you will be saved. For with the heart one believes unto righteousness, and with the mouth confession is made unto salvation. For the Scripture says, *'Whoever believes on Him will not be put to shame.'* For there is no distinction between Jew and Greek, for the same Lord over all is rich to all who call upon Him. For *'whoever calls on the name of the LORD shall be saved'*" (10:9-13).

What is extremely important to know is there is a certain violence about the Kingdom of God. Matthew says it like this: "Assuredly, I say to you, among those born of women there has not risen one greater than John the Baptist; but he who is least in the kingdom of heaven is greater than he. And from the days of John the Baptist until now the kingdom of heaven suffers violence, and the violent take it by force. For all the prophets and the law prophesied until John" (11:11-13).

Luke has this saying in another form: "The law and the prophets *were* until John. Since that time the kingdom of God has been preached, and everyone is pressing into it" (16:16).

It is clear that at some time Jesus said something in which violence and the Kingdom were connected, something which was a dark and a difficult saying, which no one at the time fully understood. Even as Luke and Matthew understood it in different ways.

Luke says that every man presses his way into the Kingdom; he means, that the Kingdom of heaven is not for the well-meaning but for the desperate. That no one drifts into the Kingdom, that the Kingdom only opens its doors to those who are prepared to make as great an effort to get into it as men do when they storm or press into a city.

Matthew says that from the time of John until now the Kingdom of heaven suffers violence and the violent take it by force. The very form of that expression seems to look back over a considerable time. It seems as though Matthew was saying from the days of John, who was thrown into prison and beheaded, right down to our own times, the Kingdom of heaven has suffered violence and persecution at the hands of violent men.

Taking both accounts of Matthew and Luke together, it is as though Jesus is saying always my Kingdom will suffer violence; always savage men will try to break it up and snatch it away and destroy it; and therefore only those who are desperately in earnest, only those in whom the violence of devotion matches and defeats the violence of persecution will in the end enter into it.

It is as though Jesus is warning his disciples of the change that would shortly come. The change that would put them through the asset test, which would be the time of tribulation and martyrdom. Think about the persecutions, first of Jesus, then his disciples even as he warned James and John when they desired to sit on either side of him, thinking he had come to set up an earthly kingdom. After Jesus put some questions to them, Jesus said: "......you will indeed drink of the cup that I drink of; and with the baptism that I am baptized withal shall ye be baptized" (Mark 10:39).

I am reminded of Lester Sumrall's book entitled, *The Militant Church*. He writes concerning the need for the "Church to be aggressive before God—Get off the defensive, and get offensive! It is time to go after the devil and go after sin." He goes on to say the devil has quickened his efforts to defeat the Church. "When we take a militant stance in the things of God such as love, prayer, the faith stance, we live in victory. Jesus being the Prince of Peace says, 'I come with a sword.'"

Jesus clarified to the religious leaders of his day that the Kingdom of God could not be found on a map relating to any particular location, here or there. It is in you; that is to say in your midst. (Luke 17:20-21) So the Kingdom of God is present wherever individual men and women have agreed that Jesus Christ is their Lord. All who regard God as their King are citizens of the Kingdom of God. So we have a Kingdom Membership, and a Church Membership.

David Oliver in his book *Church That Works,* points out that when Jesus said that He would build His Church, He set it in the context of giving the keys of the Kingdom of heaven to Peter, on whom the Church would be founded. (Mat. 16:18-19) He goes on to say; the church is set in the context of the kingdom—the rule of God through all creation—earth and heaven..... (The Kingdom) is the overarching link between the two realms, and the church is the agent by which those keys turn to open or shut, to release or bind.

The name Peter (Greek, Petros), means "rock" or "rockman." In the next phrase Christ used *petra* ("upon this rock"), a feminine form for "rock," not a name. Christ used a play on words. He does not say "upon you, Peter," or "upon your successors," but "on this rock"—upon this divine revelation and profession of faith in Christ. "I will build" shows that the formation of the church was still in the future. It began on the day of Pentecost (Acts 2). The word "church" appears in the gospels only here and in Matthew 18:17.

Who is "the Rock"? The Rock is Christ. The true church is built upon Christ: "For no other foundation can anyone lay than that which is laid, which is Jesus Christ" (1 Cor. 3:11).

So we can look at the Church as the visible manifestation of the Kingdom of God on earth, because the Kingdom of God is in us who make up the church. With this in mind we know then that the church is not defined within the four walls of a building, but the church is representative of the kingdom gathered or scattered. Therefore, whose purpose is to bring transformation to cities, regions, and nations. The issue before the church is to confront the dark powers that hold the world captive, such as death in all its manifestations, greed, hatred, war alienation, despair, fear, chaos.

The dominion of this dark kingdom has already been broken as a result of the resurrection and exaltation of Jesus Christ our Lord. The Apostle Paul writes to the Colossians in Chapter One, "giving thanks to the Father who has qualified us to be partakers of the inheritance of the saints in the light. He has delivered us from the power of darkness and conveyed *us* into the kingdom of the Son of His love, in whom we have redemption through His blood, the forgiveness of sins" (12-14). Jesus taught us to pray "Your Kingdom come, Your will be done on earth as it is in heaven" (Mat. 6:10). We argue from his power to his forgiveness, and after we have asked for the forgiveness of our sins, we plead for it on the ground, "thine is the Kingdom, and the power, and the glory."

Being Added to the Church

Being born into the Kingdom is one aspect of what happens to a new Christian upon receiving Jesus as both Christ and Lord. After being born into the Kingdom, the next step for the believer is to be added to the church. There are those who would argue that we are born in the church, or a denomination. I would ask them about those who have a Damascus Road experience as did Apostle Paul in Chapter Nine of the book of Acts, or the Ethiopian official that the angel of the Lord commanded the Evangelist Philip meet in the Gaza Desert in Chapter Eight of the same book. It is important to note that we are added to the church; but now says Apostle Paul, "has God set the members every one of them in the body, as it has pleased him" (1 Cor. 12:18).

When it comes to the church, it may vary from well-structured institutions to underground cell groups and everything in between. There are many biblical metaphors which give us insight into what the church is like, such as a family, a bride, a vineyard, a sheepfold, an army, a spiritual building, but most directly and specifically, the church is a body.

The church is the body of Christ. All the other metaphors have Old Testament equivalents, but this one does not. The concept does not even exist in the Old Testament. The body is the church's New Testament identity, as it is uniquely positioned in Christ. The church is not a physical building, but a group of believers, not a denomination, sect, or association, but a spiritual body. The church is not an organization, but an organism—a living vibrant force in the earth to advance the kingdom of God, a communion, a fellowship of one body that includes all believers.

After birth into the kingdom comes this next step for the new believer, which is to be added to a local body. The word "added" in the Greek means "to be put into, to be joined unto, to gather with a company of people." In the book of Acts we see this occurring over and over again as converts were made through the gospel. "Then those who gladly received his word were baptized; and that day about three thousand souls were added *to them*...praising God and having favor with all the people. And the Lord added to the church daily those who were being saved" (2:41/47). "And through the hands of the apostles many signs and wonders were done among the people. And they were all with one accord in Solomon's Porch. Yet none of the rest dared join them, but the people esteemed them highly. And believers were increasingly added to the Lord, multitudes of both men and women" (Acts 5:12-14).

New believers are not added to the church to be dormant or to just swell the membership. They are added to the church to be equipped, learn how to function in a corporate setting. The church being a body must have all of its members functioning in their capacity even as the natural body. As every part of our natural body has purpose, so it is as God places us in his spiritual body. In Paul's epistle to the Ephesians he writes in chapter four; "And He Himself gave some *to be* apostles, some prophets, some evangelists, and some pastors and teachers, for the equipping of the saints for the work of ministry, for the edifying of the body of Christ" (11-12).

It is the heart of the Father to have every member in the church equipped, activated, and in full function. For this to happen the Lord has supplied us with the governmental ascension of gifted men and women to teach and raise up new converts to maturity, enabling them to operate in the gift the Lord has given them for the body. There is a work of perfection taking place as Apostle Paul continues in verse twelve, "till we all come to the unity of the faith and of the knowledge of the Son of God, to a perfect man, to the measure of the stature of the fullness of Christ." What a high aim with reference to creatures so poor and needy as the members of his Church!

God has a plan. He is preparing a people with whom he can spend eternity. He is raising up a Bride for his Son. The church is being carried along according to God's preordained plan, with the goal that it will become the holy temple of God. Before this world ends, the church will fulfill its purpose, that is, "to the intent that now the manifold wisdom of God might be made known by the church to the principalities and powers in the heavenly *places,* according to the eternal purpose which He accomplished in Christ Jesus our Lord" (Eph. 3:10-11).

This does not mean that the church will take over the world. On the contrary, the world will grow more evil and wicked as we draw nearer to the end. It is when darkness covers the earth that the glory of God will shine brightest upon the church (Isa. 60:2). The church will become mightier in the Lord as the world becomes darker.

The Last Outpouring of Wine

If you want to be a part of the next move of God, then you must be willing to abandon your present wineskin. No matter how respectable, organized, nice, and stable it seems, it will not handle the next outpouring of God's Spirit. Prepare to become a part of a new wineskin.

The last outpouring of God's Spirit is going to be greater than any other. It was during the end of the Azusa Street Revival that Charles Parham prophesied on the East Coast and William Seymour prophesied on the West Coast; neither of them knew the prophecy of the other. However, both prophesied the same message, which was: The last outpouring of God's Spirit is going to be greater than any other.

Even greater than the outpouring that occurred on the Day of Pentecost.

God promised to pour out his Spirit on all flesh before the return of Jesus (Acts 2:17) *"'And it shall come to pass in the last days,' says God, 'That I will pour out of My Spirit on all flesh; Your sons and your daughters shall prophesy, Your young men shall see visions, Your old men shall dream dreams.'"*

"It is recorded that on Sunday, April 15, 1906 the Lord called me (William Seymour) to ten days of special prayer. I felt greatly burdened but had no idea of what He had particularly in mind." But Seymour said, "He had a work for me, and wanted to prepare me for it. Wednesday, April 18, the terrible San Francisco earthquake came, which also devastated the surrounding cities and country. No less than ten thousand lost their lives in San Francisco alone. I felt a deep conviction that the Lord was answering our prayers for a revival in His own way."

When Thy judgments are in the earth, the inhabitants of the world learn righteousness. (Isa. 26:9)

In this hour of the global Covid-19 Pandemic, multiple thousands around the world are dying. Families are effected emotionally, economically, socially in measures we have never experienced in modern times. It seems to me God is shouting to individuals and his church to draw closer to Him than we've ever been before. And yet there is an indifference to his voice as many struggle to attempt to continue as usual without any adjustment to their social or spiritual lives. But in spite of man's attitude, God will have a church, and a people in these last days who will move in great authority and power in the earth realm. Amen!

TWO

Being Used by God

In your goodness you let the blind speak of your light.
NICHOLAS OF CUSA

*And all of us, as with unveiled face, [because we]
continued to behold [in the Word of God] as in a mirror
the glory of the Lord, are constantly being transfigured
into His very own image in ever increasing splendor and
from one degree of glory to another; [for this comes]
from the Lord [Who is] the Spirit.*
2 CORINTHIANS 3:18 (AMP)

As it was with Moses, Gideon, Jeremiah, let's not forget
Esther and Deborah; as a matter of fact all whom God
used were acutely aware of their insufficiency. Most
of us, like our ancestors, struggled with the "how am I going
to accomplish this assignment?!" syndrome. We read about
them in Scripture and look at them as giants in the Spirit.
And they were! Because they learned how to be used under
the influence of the anointing of God.

Today in many ways, God still speaks to us as he used to

speak to our ancestors at a time when there were neither spiritual directors nor any systems of spirituality. To be faithful to the designs of God then comprised the whole of one's spiritual life. To be devoted to the Lord God had not become a science crammed with precepts and detailed instructions. It seems that nowadays, our special needs make this necessary, but in the old days people were less complex and more straightforward.

In this second apostolic age in which we live today, I think we are finally beginning to understand that we are not the ones who do the calling; it is God. Leaders, denominations, theological educators, etc. can't make apostles, prophets, evangelist, pastors, teachers, or saints. The Lord calls who he chooses in spite of our assessment of the individual called, or even our own position in Christ. Who would have thought the Lord would have considered them? As my wife Pearlie shared with me concerning her calling in the Lord, "I thought the whole world was really in trouble when I heard the voice of the Lord." Well I didn't think it was quite that bad, but I certainly had some questions.

There is a reason why we shrink back in hesitation as we receive the calling to service from the Lord. It is because we are aware of our insufficiency in our own ability to accomplish the assignment given by the Lord. This thinking is because God has selected for His purpose the foolish things of the world to shame the wise and reveal their ignorance. And God has selected for His purpose the weak things of the world to shame the things which are strong to reveal their frailty. God has selected for his purpose the insignificant things of the world, and the things that are despised and treated with contempt, even the things that are nothing, so that no one will be able to boast in the presence of God.

The Sanhedrin Council looked down on the apostles as "unlearned and ignorant men" (Acts 4:13). But they were amazed at their boldness, and what being with Jesus had done for them. The apostles were for the most part fisherman, carpenters, common men; but chosen by our Lord such as many of us are today.

This quotation with which Paul finishes this passage is from Jeremiah 9:23-24—"Thus says the LORD: 'Let not the wise *man* glory in his wisdom, Let not the mighty *man* glory in his might, Nor let the rich *man* glory in his riches; But let him who glories glory in this, That he understands and knows Me, That I *am* the LORD, exercising loving-kindness, judgment, and righteousness in the earth. For in these I delight,' says the LORD."

It is said the one basic sin is self-assertion, or the desire for recognition. It is only when we realize that we can do nothing and that God can and will do everything that real religion begins. It is the amazing fact of life that it is the people who realize their own weakness and their own lack of wisdom, who in the end are strong and wise. It is the fact of experience that the man who thinks that he can take on life all by himself is certain in the end to make shipwreck.

Watchman Nee in his book, *A Table in the Wilderness,* states that, "The cross is the greatest leveler in the universe. It brings every one of us to zero. It offers the whole of mankind a new beginning. The difference between a Christian who progresses fast and one who progresses slowly is in the faithfulness and obedience of the former, never in anything he possesses by nature."

There are many things too strong and too imposing for God to use. Instead he not only chooses the weak things and the despised, he goes further. The apostle seems almost at a loss to know how to define the things, so weak and despicable in men's eyes, that God elects to use. In a telling phrase he sums them up as the "things which are not."

So as we walk with Him, we come to know God wants useable instruments who will carry the mystery, the weight of glory and the burden of sin simultaneously, who can bear the darkness and the light, who can hold the paradox of incarnation—flesh and spirit, human and divine, joy and suffering, at the same time, just as Jesus did. In essence, watch what Jesus does, and do the same thing! That of course is a process.

To What Purpose Was the Ten Commandments?

God gave Israel the Ten Commandments and said to them "if thou art willing to keep the commandments, and to keep the faith, that pleases me and they shall preserve thee." "If thou art willing to keep" proves there's a will in man to keep or not to keep; otherwise, what is the sense of saying to him who has no will, "if thou will?" It would seem ridiculous to say to a blind man, "if thou are willing to see, you will find a treasure." Or to a deaf man, "if thou art willing to hear, I will tell thee a good story." That would seem to be mocking their misery, and having a gross disregard for their infirmity.

Yet this represents human reasoning and thinking which pulls the Scriptures of God the direction we choose. Human wisdom is absurd, and stupid, and will always miss the holy things of God. "'For my thoughts *are* not your thoughts, neither *are* your ways my ways,' saith the LORD. 'For *as* the heavens are higher than the earth, so are my ways higher than your ways, and my thoughts than your thoughts'" (Isaiah 55:8-9).

When God says, "if thou art willing," "if thou shalt do," "if thou shall hear," it is not an act of mockery to the impotent. How often do parents play with their children, bidding them come to them, or do this or that, only in order that it may appear how impotent they are, and that they may be compelled to call for the help of the parent's hand? How often does a faithful physician tell an obstinate patient to do or stop doing things that are impossible or injurious to him, so as to bring him by experience of himself to a knowledge of his disease or weakness, to which he cannot lead him by any other course? And what is more common and widespread than to use insulting and provoking language when we would show our enemies or friends what they can and cannot do?

God, as a father, deals with us as with His sons, with a view to showing us the impotence of which we are ignorant; or as a faithful physician, with a view to making known to us our disease; or if, to taunt His enemies, who proudly resist his counsel and the laws he has set forth, He may say: "do," "hear," "keep," or: "if thou shalt hear," "if thou art willing," "if thou shalt do." God is not mocking us, but rather God is trying us, that by his law he may bring us to a knowledge of our impotence, if we are his friends. Or else, he is really and deservedly taunting and mocking us, if we are his proud enemies.

For this Paul teaches in Galatians: "Wherefore then *serveth* the law? It was added because of transgressions, till the seed should come to whom the promise was made; *and it was* ordained by angels in the hand of a mediator...Wherefore the law was our schoolmaster *to bring us* unto Christ, that we might be justified by faith. But after that faith is come, we are no longer under a schoolmaster. For ye are all the children of God by faith in Christ Jesus" (3:19/24-26).

Human nature is blind, so that it does not know its own

strength—or, rather its sickness; moreover being proud, it thinks it knows and can do everything. God can cure this pride and ignorance by no readier remedy than the publication of His law.

Are You a Mentor or Mentee?

And if he have not been faithful in that which is another man's, who shall give you that which is your own? (Luke 16:12)

This Scripture seems to have a double meaning as on one hand it relates to our stewardship in the earth regarding the property of our Lord. Here we have our earthly possessions plainly spoken of as the goods of another, that is, of God, and of these goods we are but the temporary stewards. Although on earth man can possess nothing of his own—here he is but a steward for a time of property belonging to another—yet a prospect is held out to him that, if he be found faithful in the trust while on earth, in the world to come something will be given to him really and truly his own.

So it is as you desire to perfect that ministry God has given you. There comes the time you must be faithful to serve in another man's ministry. You must become that protégé to one who is already established so you can develop faithfulness in and through your service. And in so doing the skills, the wisdom, the patience, needed for leadership will be developed in you. The Apostle Paul told Timothy, "the things that thou hast heard of me among many witnesses, the same commit thou to faithful men, who shall be able to teach others also" (2 Timothy 2:2).

I am a second generational leader succeeding my father, the late Bishop James A. Dockery, having been raised in the church along with my five other brothers and sisters. All of us were called to ministry and were mentored or discipled by our father for various periods of time. I remained with my father because somehow I knew I was not supposed to leave his side. Having received offers to pastor in other areas, I still had no leading to leave my father's side. As such I remember how conscious he was to keep me close, especially as he met with various leaders and colleagues regarding all kinds of ministry issues. There was such a relationship between my dad and I, the Lord birthed within me the continuation of the ministry vision before my father went home. And of course since, the Lord has brought it to pass.

The Old Testament consists of men, women, kings, prophets, judges, and military leaders, who followed the plan of God mentoring and leading people that he ordained to use in his kingdom. The Spirit of the Lord initiated the mentoring duties by Moses, Elijah, and Deborah (Deut. 31:8-9; 2 Kings 2:9-13; Judg. 4:3-7). God instructed Moses to make Joshua his successor over the people of Israel and lead them to the Promised Land (Num. 27:18-19). God told Elijah to anoint Elisha as a prophet in his place (1 Kings 19:16). Deborah's prophecy from God was to deploy Barak and his troops to fight Jabin's army (Judg. 4:6-7).

These were leaders who sought followers that "God chose" to support the plans of his kingdom. In Num. 27:18-23, God called Moses to transfer his spirit as the leader of Israel to Joshua. God told Elijah to anoint Elisha to the status of a prophet as his replacement (1 Kings 19:16). God delivered the prophecy to Deborah that Barak followed, defeating the Canaanite enemy who was oppressing the children of Israel (Judg. 4:1-9).

I remember so vividly when my dad came to me and told me the Lord spoke to him, saying: "I want you to make your son Billy, your assistant bishop." At that time I was about thirty-two years old, accomplished some Bible School, and saw myself as a novice in comparison to many of my colleagues. We had an organization of about fifteen churches whose leaders were well tested and primarily seniors in ministry. It was at a time the assistant bishop originally with my father was a senior pastor and superintendent, I would say in his sixties. But he died suddenly, therefore leaving the need to appoint his replacement.

When my dad approached me to share the news of the position, I immediately refused to accept it, citing the fact that he should give the position to the senior leaders who I knew sought it. That night I had a visitation from the Lord that shook me to my very core. As I laid in bed not giving the position another thought, I received a vision from the Lord—it was as though His arm came out of heaven with a huge Bible in his hand saying, "TAKE IT, THE POSITION IS YOURS." I knew then that my father came to me not just because I was his son, but in obedience to the Lord.

God called Moses to commission Joshua to take the leadership position amid the congregation (Num. 27:15-23). Moses placed some of his honor on Joshua, who had the spirit of leadership on him. Moses laid his hands on Joshua, filling him with the spirit of wisdom to lead the children of Israel. Joshua began leading the people so that they would obey him as their transformational leader by shifting their mindset, their approaches, and their methodology. As a transitional leader he removed the old design through reorganization. Joshua did not compromise but followed the voice of God, successfully leading a different generation to inhabit the Promised Land.

God also called Elijah, (a transformational leader), to be His prophet (1 Kings 17:18). He is one without a father being mentioned, traveling from city to city, relying on Father God as his source of strength to guide him. Elijah turned the heart of the people back to God with a victory on Mount Carmel where the fire of God consumed the altar and all that was on it and the water around it (1 Kings 18:37, 38). After Elijah's victory on Mount Carmel, Jezebel vowed to kill him, so he ran to a mountain complaining to God that he was the only prophet left (1 Kings 18, 19). God strengthened Elijah, initiating a God transformation by sending Elijah to anoint Jehu as king and Elisha to succeed him as a prophet (1 Kings 19:15).

Deborah was a leader who served in three leadership positions—as a prophetess (Judg. 4:4, 5), a Judge (Judg. 4:4-14), and a military strategist (Judg. 4:6-7, 9). Deborah had spiritual and political leadership qualities like no other female recorded in Scripture. She was a developmental leader who supervised Israel's dilemma of anguish by Jabin, king of Canaan. Deborah attained a solution to combat Israel's oppression using her gift as prophetess and role as Judge to transform Israel from defeat to success. As a woman in the Old Testament, Deborah is a transitional leader, removing the old design of male leadership and developing a model of female leadership. It is said that Deborah's position as a Judge was an "image of accord" because the people came to her for decisions. As judge and deliverer of Israel, she was a liberator, who called the people to worship God (Judg. 5:2-3, 9). The people of Israel credited Deborah and Barak with obedience to God's Word, and the land had rest for forty years (Judg. 5:2, 31). God's victory over the Canaanites through Deborah and Barak was the final blow to the Canaanite nation.

We don't know why in this period of Israel's lifetime, the women (Deborah and Jael) had to enter the fight to defeat the Canaanites. But Deborah did not hesitate to do what God ordained. Barak would not fight unless Deborah accompanied the men into battle. Even so Deborah went with the ten thousand men and Barak to battle the Canaanites (Judg. 4:7-22).

All Fruitfulness Flows from God

We look at Jesus for example, after He was tempted in the Wilderness of Judea, returned to Nazareth, went into the synagogue on the Sabbath Day, and He was handed the Book, opened to where it said: *"'The Spirit of the LORD is upon Me, Because He has anointed Me To preach the gospel to the poor; He has sent Me to heal the brokenhearted, To proclaim liberty to the captives And recovery of sight to the blind, To set at liberty those who are oppressed; To proclaim the acceptable year of the LORD.'* Then He closed the book, and gave *it* back to the attendant and sat down. And the eyes of all who were in the synagogue were fixed on Him" (Luke 4:18-20).

Nazareth was the place where Jesus grew up; it was the place of His education. He returned there after being tested in the wilderness. The people there could barely recognize Him because of the anointing, the power of God upon Him. But we are made aware of why He could not stay in Nazareth, "And leaving Nazareth, He came and dwelt in Capernaum, which is by the sea, in the regions of Zebulun and Naphtali, that it might be fulfilled which was spoken by Isaiah the prophet, saying: *The land of Zebulun and the land of Naphtali, By the way of the sea, beyond the Jordan, Galilee of the Gentiles: The people who sat in darkness have seen a*

*great light, And upon those who sat in the region and shadow
of death Light has dawned"'* (Mat. 4:13-16).

It was to Capernaum the prophets prophesied He would
go; the place of His ordinary residence, the focus of His
preaching and miracles, "So He got into a boat, crossed
over, and came to His own city" (Mat 9:1). Bethlehem was
the place of His birth, Nazareth the place of His education,
Capernaum the place of His Ministry, Jerusalem the place of
His death. You see, when the glory of the Lord is upon your
life, you operate in His capacity and His realm.

This is what you cannot discern if you have no inner experience of how the Spirit works in your own life. You will just
substitute the text for the real inner Spirit, or as the Apostle
Paul says, "The written letter alone will bring death, but the
Spirit gives life" (2 Cor. 3:6). It is critical that we understand
God is not dependent upon our knowledge in the sense that
the western mind, or we in the United States understand
knowledge. We live in a world where ninety-eight percent
of the people who have ever lived could not read or write. So
God's dealing with man would be more akin to face-to-face
presence, full body knowing or intimacy, rather than external preparation such as Bible School, Seminary, or our ability
to pursue Him through our senses.

The Lord said to me in a dream concerning those who have
come to Him, "many are married to me, but they have not
consummated the marriage." There is a difference between
belief system and living faith. We move from one to the other
only by the power of the Holy Spirit who is the stable witness within. He is the one who leads us and guides us into all
truth, and tells us things to come.

Consummation represents the process of making a marriage or relationship complete. It is the moment when some-

thing is finished or consummated. The consummation of a year's hard work might be when you use your earnings to finally achieve your dream. When it comes to our relationship with the Lord, consummation can only happen through encounter, surrender, trust and obedience. It is only through intimacy that vision, purpose, and destiny is birthed. This can only happen in the Secret Place:

He who dwells in the secret place of the Most High Shall abide under the shadow of the Almighty. I will say of the LORD, "*He is* my refuge and my fortress; My God, in Him I will trust." (Psalm 91:1-2)

Because he has set his love upon Me, therefore I will deliver him; I will set him on high, because he has known My name. He shall call upon Me, and I will answer him; I *will be* with him in trouble; I will deliver him and honor him. With long life I will satisfy him, And show him My salvation. (Psalms 91:14-16)

Abide in Me, and I in you. As the branch cannot bear fruit of itself, unless it abides in the vine, neither can you, unless you abide in Me. I am the vine, you *are* the branches. He who abides in Me, and I in him, bears much fruit; for without Me you can do nothing. (John 15:4-5)

These words remind us that it is God who has placed us in Christ. We are there, and we are told to stay there! It was God's own act, and we are to abide by it. "Abide in me, and I in you." This is a double sentence: a command matched by a promise. There is an objective and a subjective side to God's working, and the subjective depends on the objective; the "I in you" is the outcome of our abiding in him. We need to guard against being overanxious about the subjective side of things, as though a branch of the vine should strive to produce grapes of a particular size or color. We need to dwell upon the objective—"Abide in Me"—and let God take care of the outcome. And this He has undertaken to do. The character of the fruit is always determined by the vine.

How often is it only at the point of utter despair with ourselves that we remember the Lord, and relinquish to Him the task he is so ready and able to perform! The sooner we do so the better, for while we monopolize it we leave little room for the Spirit's mighty working. You see, the object of temptation is always to get us to do something. Satan knows well that as soon as we step out of our Hiding Place, as soon as we move from the cover of Christ and act in self-dependence, he has scored a victory.

I'm not writing to you to tell you something you don't already know, but to second the motion to what God has already place within you. "Before I formed you in the womb I knew you; Before you were born I sanctified you; I ordained you a prophet to the nations" (Jer. 1:5). "Your eyes saw my substance, being yet unformed. And in Your book they all were written, The days fashioned for me, When *as yet there were* none of them" (Ps. 139:16). "Listen, O coastlands, to Me, And take heed, you peoples from afar! The LORD has called Me from the womb; From the matrix of My mother He has made mention of My name" (Is. 49:1).

Even Peter the apostle said that his work was by and large "recalling," "reminding" the people. "For this reason I will not be negligent to remind you always of these things, though you know and are established in the present truth.

Yes, I think it is right, as long as I am in this tent, to stir you up by reminding *you,* knowing that shortly I *must* put off my tent, just as our Lord Jesus Christ showed me. Moreover I will be careful to ensure that you always have a reminder of these things after my decease" (2 Peter 1:12-15).

When preachers and teachers do not realize that in most cases they are reminding, recalling, or stirring up the people of God, we take ourselves far too seriously, and it causes believers to rely more on external authority than their own inner authority and development in Christ.

When Plato writes of Socrates as a "midwife," he tells the story about the relationship between teacher and student, about education, and about the birth of spiritual—intellectual fire in the soul. This speaks to the fact that they are both interested in the transformative practice of helping people give birth to their true self. Socrates famously used the metaphor of philosopher as midwife to help explain his particularly unique approach to philosophy. Three times Peter speaks of his desire to remind his readers of the truth that was already in them. This speaks to the fact that, on some level spiritual cognition—that is what God has placed within us in terms of insight, perception, and discernment. Our image and likeness of Him becomes "re-cognition" as we are taught by teachers and preachers called by God. In essence, spiritual preachers and teachers become midwives as critical birthing takes place, bringing forth the treasure in us. Actually when we understand our purpose; isn't that responsibility placed on each of us in the Body of Christ as we interact, to encourage, inspire, edify, exhort and comfort one another?

Pursue love, and desire spiritual *gifts,* but especially that you may prophesy. For he who speaks in a tongue does not speak to men but to God, for no one understands *Him;* however, in the spirit he speaks mysteries. But he who prophesies speaks edification and exhortation and comfort to men. (1 Corinthians 14:1-3)

Amen!

THREE

One God

You shall have no other gods before or besides Me.
EXODUS 20:3 (AMP)

O ne way to read the entire Bible is to be conscious of the gradual unveiling of our faces in terms of clarity and relationship with the Lord. The gradual movement of our very being as we advance, from infants, to teenage love, to infatuation, to adult communion with God. The Word of God can bring us to a place in our relationship with God where we can both receive the love of God and experience the flow of His love from ourselves to others. This love that flows out from us will only be an extension of who we have come to be in God. A love that will also cause the lives of others to be transformed in a way that even their lives will impact the lives of others.

In many ways what we're seeing as we explore the Bible is an observing of the development of human consciousness and human readiness for God. That's why we see some difference between the earlier and later Scriptures. There's been development in consciousness. In short, we start with tribal thinking, and then we gradually move toward individual thinking, through the dialogue of election (the act of choosing), failure, and grace.

For example, Ezekiel spoke the word of the Lord saying, "'the fathers have eaten sour grapes, and the children's teeth are set on edge" (Ezek 18:2) Meaning, if the father of the family sins, the entire family bares the consequence of that fault. *God goes on to say,* "you shall no longer use this proverb in Israel because, all souls are mine; the soul of the father as well as the soul of the son is mine; the soul who sins shall die...Again, when a wicked *man* turns away from the wickedness which he committed, and does what is lawful and right, he preserves himself alive. Because he considers and turns away from all the transgressions which he committed, he shall surely live; he shall not die" (Ezek. 18:3-4, 18:27-28).

In these parts of Scripture we actually see the shift as the Lord speaks to Ezekiel that the responsibility of obedience to God would no longer be tribal, clannish, or tied to a family. Each individual will be responsible for their own actions whether they would be to their punishment or to their reward with God.

When we consider the earlier Scriptures we vividly see the result of tribalism, clan, and family because everyone connected to an individual's behavior suffered the consequences. For example, Achan forsook obeying the command of God, because he took the spoils of Jericho after its defeat. The result was terrifying because his sons, his daughters, his oxen, his donkeys, his sheep, his tent, and all that he had, was taken to the Valley of Achor and stoned by all Israel. (Josh. 7:22-25)

This speaks to the fact that there comes a time we really need to separate ourselves from the familiar if we are going to truly follow the Lord. There are those who miss God because of the actions of those they are associated with. In other words, their service to God is based upon a particular group of people, a tradition or comfort zone as opposed to a personal relationship with the Savior. Hebrews 11:5 says: "By faith Enoch was taken away so that he did not see death, *'and was not found, because God had taken him';* for before he was taken he had this testimony, that he pleased God." In Genesis 5:24, we see that "Enoch walked with God; and he *was* not, for God took him." It is amazing the kind of relationship we can develop with the Lord by being single-minded. Look at Job's character in relationship with God, as he used him to prove a point to the devil—Job was blameless and upright, and one who feared God and shunned evil.

It is our individual faith stance, and our individual diligence in seeking God, that enables us to please the Lord and be rewarded by him. (Heb. 11:6) In this life we are not able to achieve union with God through our intellect, our imagination, or through any of our senses. We can only achieve this union by faith, by hope, and by love. The state of self-abandonment is a blending of faith, hope, and love in one single act which unites us to God and all His activities.

When we see Moses on Mount Sinai, he says to God, "'Show me your glory, I beg you.' And God says, 'I will let all my splendor pass in front of you, and I will pronounce before you the name of the Lord before you. But I have compassion on whom I will. I show pity to whom I please. You are not ready to see my face. For humanity cannot see me and live.' And so God says to him, 'There is a place in the cleft of the rock; stand there. When my glory passes by, I will shield you with my hand while I pass by. Then I will take my hand away and you will see the back of me. But my face you cannot see'" (Ex. 33:18-22).

In the beginning of our relationship with the Lord, a mature adult relationship with Him is not yet possible. However, as we continue in the Lord—by the end of the Bible, we're going to have a perfectly personal face-to-face relationship, but it is going to take us a long time to get there, just as it does with each of us individually. It seems the experience of specialness is almost too awesome to be carried by an individual. One will either disbelieve it or abuse it, either by ego deflation or ego inflation, which is self-hatred or conceit. We see, and even may have experienced how difficult it is for a person to stand before the face of God, and the people of God in that perfect balance between humility and dignity. Look at Saul's pride—He took it upon himself to act as priest (1 Sam. 13:8-14). He blatantly disobeyed a command from the Lord. (1 Sam. 15) Even though he sought to justify his disobedience by saying he purposed to sacrifice to the Lord, he still placed his will ahead of God's.

The Church would be much more proficient and powerful in its ability to carry out its mandate in the earth, which is to bring many souls into the Kingdom of God, if it were not for pride and insecurity.

So God begins with a people consecrated as his very own—"You *are* the children of the LORD your God; you shall not cut yourselves nor shave the front of your head for the dead. For you *are* a holy people to the LORD your God, and the LORD has chosen you to be a people for Himself, a special treasure above all the peoples who *are* on the face of the earth" (Deut. 14:1-2).

The group or tribe holds the mystery together ("And without controversy great is the mystery of godliness: God was manifest in the flesh, justified in the Spirit, seen of angels, preached unto the Gentiles, believed on in the world, received up into glory" (1 Timothy 3:16)), which becomes the very meaning of "Church." Membership in the group will become a gateway to being added to the church where we learn personal growth, relationships with one another and intimacy with the Lord. But so often the institution itself becomes a substitute for personal encounter and inner experience because we love the organization more than the organism, which I would call the Spirit Life of the Church. So when we are delinquent in our behavior with God, it reflects on everything concerning our life. How we relate to God always reveals how we will relate to people, and how we relate to people is an almost infallible indicator of how we relate to God and let God relate to us. How we relate, is how we relate, and how we relate to anything is a good indicator of how we relate to everything. The whole Bible is a school on relationship, revealing both its best qualities and its worst.

No Other Gods Before "Me"

We must begin with God. All our words and works must be characterized by the first words of the Bible: "In the beginning God." Nothing is right that does not begin with Him. "God first" is the voice of Scripture. "Seek ye first the kingdom of God and His righteousness; and all these things shall be added unto you" (Matt. 6:33) is the testimony of Jesus. "God first" is the great proclamation. The angels sang: "Glory to God in the highest." This was the beginning of their song. And it was after this that they sang of "good-will" towards men. We cannot give glory to God without doing good to men.

The rapid decline, which is the great mark of these last days, comes from ignoring the fact that God is first. The Gospel of our Lord, as the Apostle Paul wrote: "For I am not ashamed of the gospel of Christ: for it is the power of God unto salvation to everyone that believeth; to the Jew first, and also to the Greek" (Romans 1:16). This Gospel is being rapidly and almost universally superseded by the gospel of man, which is a gospel of sanitation and is now openly called "Christian Socialism" without Christ. It is a gospel that begins with man; its object is to improve the old nature apart from God, and to reform the flesh; and the measure of its success is the measure in which man can become "good" without "God."

> For my thoughts *are* not your thoughts, neither *are* your ways my ways," saith the LORD. "For *as* the heavens are higher than the earth, so are my ways higher than your ways, and my thoughts than your thoughts. (Isaiah 55:8-9)

Man's ways and thoughts are the opposite of God's. God says, "Seek First." Man says, "Take care of number one," and his great aim is to be independent of God.

Independence, in God, is His glory. Independence in man, is his sin, and rebellion, and shame.

In the Word of God, God is first and before all.

> ......before me there was no God formed, neither shall there be after me. I, *even* I, *am* the LORD; and beside me *there is* no saviour. (Isaiah 43:10-11)

> Thus saith the LORD the King of Israel, and his redeemer the LORD of hosts; "I *am* the first, and I *am* the last; and beside me *there is* no God." (Isaiah 44:6)

Hearken unto me, O Jacob and Israel, my called; I *am* he; I *am* the first, I also *am* the last. Mine hand also hath laid the foundation of the earth, and my right hand hath spanned the heavens: *when* I call unto them, they stand up together. (Isaiah 48:12-13)

I am Alpha and Omega, the beginning and the ending, saith the Lord, which is, and which was, and which is to come, the Almighty. (Rev. 1:8, 1:11, 1:17, 22:13)

This is the great truth emphasized by the Word of God. When it is not heeded there is confusion, deception, and sorrow. When it is received there is joy, peace, and contentment.

When God says, "No gods before me," he is saying, literally, "before my face," a Hebrew idiom, and equivalent to "beside me," in addition to, "to me." The commandment requires the worship of one God alone—Jehovah, the God who in so many ways manifested Himself to the Israelites and us, and implies that there is, in point and fact, no other.

Our soul must be for God only, all else is emptiness and falsehood. There must be nothing even of our holy things put between the soul and God. His presence must be the very life and air we breathe. This demand is fulfilled by keeping ourselves from idols. Caution must be taken as our daily actions, our interests, affections, pleasures, may lead to our esteeming something our chief goal instead of God.

Israel understood it this way: "No foreign god in opposition to me." The natural idea is that Jehovah was one among many deities, that possibly away from Egypt some other god may have higher authority—such as what we see King Hezekiah confronted with in Judah:

Has any of the gods of the nations at all delivered its
land from the hand of the king of Assyria? Where *are*
the gods of Hamath and Arpad? Where *are* the gods
of Sepharvaim and Hena and Ivah? Indeed, have they
delivered Samaria from my hand? Who among all the
gods of the lands have delivered their countries from
my hand, that the LORD should deliver Jerusalem
from my hand? (2 Kings 18:33-35)

The nation of Judah was sandwiched between two world
powers, Egypt and Assyria. Both wanted to control Judah and
Israel because they lay at the vital crossroads of all Middle
Eastern trade. The nation who controlled Judah would have
a military and economic advantage over its rivals. When
Hezekiah became king, Assyria controlled Judah. Acting
with great courage, Hezekiah rebelled against this mighty
empire to who his father had submitted. He placed his faith
in God's strength rather than his own, and he obeyed God's
commands in spite of the obstacles and dangers that, from a
purely human standpoint, looked overwhelming.

Only when we are able to put our trust in God are we able to
experience the miracle of monotheism. Serving one God is not
only a gift to spirituality; it is a gift to our mental and emotional
health. Somehow "one God" tells us that there is one coherent,
or logical world. This gives order and connection. The genius
of the first commandment is, by putting "one God before you,"
you were placed inside of one coherent world, with one center,
one pattern, one realm of meaning. Having one who confirms
us is a very good start for our structure and growth as persons.
God for the believer becomes the ultimate constituting other;
this makes perfect sense because of the creation of man. God
made us in His image and after His likeness (Gen. 1:26).

And what is even more powerful as well, John says we are chosen to be friends of God, as opposed to servants, as long as we are obedient to His commandments. Jesus continues in pointing out the fact that we did not choose Him but He chose us to be fruitful (John 15:14-16). Paul says we were chosen even before the foundation of the world—that the God and Father of our Lord Jesus Christ has blessed us with every spiritual blessing in the heavenly *places* in Christ, that we should be holy and without blame before Him in love (Eph. 1:3-4).

In so much that we are human, without some significant other naming us, we have a very fragile sense of ourselves. Having many gods before us is like a state of sexual promiscuity; the person remains scattered, dissipated, without focus and like a "reed shaking in the wind." This is particularly true in today's society. Without a significant other who is also The Significant Other, we are burdened with being our own center and circumference. That's probably impossible and finally futile if you try. If this is the case our center will change every few hours, or every few minutes, with every new celebrity, image name, TV show, or magazine— constantly the untransformed self will suffer the confusion of image consciousness.

I write to you that you may know the One True God, and be filled with the riches of His Grace. These five Scriptures give insight to our creator's desire concerning us as He draws us to Himself:

Do not love the world or the things in the world. If anyone loves the world, the love of the Father is not in him. For all that *is* in the world—the lust of the flesh, the lust of the eyes, and the pride of life—is not of the

Father but is of the world. And the world is passing away, and the lust of it; but he who does the will of God abides forever. (1 John 2:15-17)

"Teacher, which *is* the great commandment in the law?" Jesus said to him, *"You shall love the LORD your God with all your heart, with all your soul, and with all your mind."* This is *the* first and great commandment. And *the* second *is* like it: *"You shall love your neighbor as yourself."* On these two commandments hang all the Law and the Prophets. (Mat. 22:36-40)

No one can serve two masters; for either he will hate the one and love the other, or else he will be loyal to the one and despise the other. You cannot serve God and mammon. (Mat. 6:24)

Adulterers and adulteresses! Do you not know that friendship with the world is enmity with God? Whoever therefore wants to be a friend of the world makes himself an enemy of God. (James 4:4)

For do I now persuade men, or God? Or do I seek to please men? For if I still pleased men, I would not be a bondservant of Christ. But I make known to you, brethren that the gospel which was preached by me is not according to man. For I neither received it from man, nor was I taught *it*, but *it came* through the revelation of Jesus Christ. (Gal. 1:10-12)

The Face of the Other

The French philosopher Emanuel Levinas thought on human sociality, which means that ethically people are responsible to one another in the face-to-face encounter. "The face of the other" that transforms us and gives us our deepest identity. The face of God for Moses, the face of Rebecca (a lover) for Jacob, the face of the prophet Nathan for David, the face of Delilah for Samson. The faces of the other concerning these individuals changed their truth.

We really are socially contagious human beings, but we settle for "human doings." It is at the being level that life is most vitally transferred. That's what happened to each one of us when we first fell in love—that's why falling in love is so exciting. Suddenly the very eyes of the other receiving me, delighting in me, enjoying me and looking at me, make me feel like me, and my best me!

The lover can say that "it's as if I never knew myself until you knew me," or "it's as if I never could accept myself until you accepted me." That's how fragile we are and how needy we are of one another's love and affirmation. How much power God has given us for one another! We've been given the capacity to receive one another's love and to receive one another's curse, to affirm one another and to deny one another, and these become the very gateways for divine affirmation or ignorance of the divine. Yet even as there is always some who will reject you, even as they have rejected our Lord and Savior, His arms are stretched out to us saying—"Come to me, all *you* who labor and are heavy laden, and I will give you rest. Take my yoke upon you and learn from me, I am gentle and lowly in heart, and you will find rest for your souls. For my yoke *is* easy and my burden is light" (Mat. 11:28-30).

For believers, that is also what happens when they apprehend the "Real Presence" of Jesus. We move to a deeper level of being ourselves when we genuinely receive and encounter the power and the presence in the gaze of the Lord Jesus Christ. There is a gradual transfiguration, a mystical and spiritual change which is produced in us while we contemplate Christ. Our spiritual assimilation to Christ comes from his glory and issues in a glory like his from strength to strength.

Before there is an enlightenment by the Spirit of the Lord, scales are upon our eyes and the veil is before our countenance. But, in Heaven's light we see light. The sin, the prejudice, the unbelief, which hid the Savior from our view, have been removed, and nothing comes between the soul and its Savior.

Instead of the countenance being concealed by a veil, it is, in the case of true Christians, converted into a mirror, which receives and then reflects the rays of light. As the believer sets their affections on things above, the glory of the Lord—that same glory that raised our Redeemer—is gathered up and given forth by the renewed and purified character of the believer.

Faith in Christ and fellowship with Christ are the forces which produce assimilation to Christ. The image which is beheld seems to fix itself upon the mirror-like soul that receives it. The life of faith serves to carry on a gradual process of spiritual assimilation. The progression is denoted by the phrase, "from glory to glory," by which we understand, not earthly splendor, but spiritual excellence and perfection. And the agency is indicated by the expression here used, "as by the Spirit of the Lord." Because he is the Spirit, the Lord has access to the heart, and renews, hallows, and glorifies the nature to which he makes himself graciously and divinely known. And there is no limit to this process of unveiling, it is as though we walk out of time into eternity. The Bible states by faith Enoch walked with God; he was taken away, for he did not see death. We know there is a crossing over from this life to eternal life. When we allow the unveiling of our face to bring about a face-to-face relationship with the Lord, it is as though the process of moving from glory to glory is only a continuation into the Throne Room of Heaven.

In the first book of John, John writes, "Behold what manner of love the Father has bestowed on us, that we should be called children of God! Therefore the world does not know us, because it did not know Him. Beloved, now we are children of God; and it has not yet been revealed what we shall be, but we know that when He is revealed, we shall be like Him, for we shall see Him as He is. And everyone who has this hope in Him purifies himself, just as He is pure" (3:1-3).

God's Love

In words which can still bring tears to the eyes, St. Augustine describes the desolation into which the death of his friend Nebridius plunged him (Confessions 1V, 10). Then he draws a moral. This is what comes, he says, of giving one's heart to anything but God. All human beings pass away. Do not let your happiness depend on something you may lose. If love is to be a blessing, not a misery, it must be for the only Beloved who will never pass away.

Jesus says, "Do not lay up for yourselves treasures on earth, where moth and rust destroy and where thieves break in and steal; but lay up for yourselves treasures in heaven, where neither moth nor rust destroys and where thieves do not break in and steal. For where your treasure is, there your heart will be also...No one can serve two masters; for either he will hate the one and love the other, or else he will be loyal to the one and despise the other. You cannot serve God and mammon" (Mat. 6:19-21, 6:24).

The whole man must be given to God. It is the heart God asks for, give me your heart, he says to each of us. The heart will be where the treasure is. Where is our treasure, our chief good, the object of our strongest desires? If it is on earth, it will fail us, we will eventually lose it. "I must leave all this! I must leave all this!" was the sad cry of the great French statesman, Cardinal Mzarin, when, stricken already by the hand of death, he took his last view of the treasures of art, and the costly adornments of his earthly home. God bids us trust our precious things to him. He is able to keep that which we have committed unto him against that day (2 Tim. 1:12). He ask it for our sake; it is safe in his keeping. Then lay up for yourselves treasure in heaven—the treasure of holy thoughts, holy aspirations, holy deeds. Above all, let Christ himself be the Treasure, the dearest Possession of our hearts, the Joy of our souls. Earthly treasures are but as dross to those who win Christ, the heavenly Treasure. If our treasure is heavenly, our hearts will become heavenly too—filled with heavenly affections, heavenly hopes; and this hope will not make you ashamed.

Our gift to God must be entire, and our surrender to God must be complete. "God spoke these words, and said, 'I am the Lord thy God: thou shalt have none other gods but me.'" It was the first of the commandments of Mount Sinai; the Lord repeats it from the Mount of the Beatitudes. There are two masters who divide the allegiance of mankind. Some serve the living and true God; some serve mammon—riches, earthly things. No man can serve both; it is impossible. The heart cannot be divided between the two; its most chief affection must be set on one great center. Those who set their love on mammon will end in hating God. Friendship with the world is an enemy, hostility and animosity to God (James 4:4). He who clings to Father God, the heavenly Treasure, will despise the good things of this world. There is nothing upon earth that he desires in comparison with God. To serve mammon is to desert the true God, to set up an idol in the heart. Scripture gives us to know that covetousness is idolatry. There is a choice every man must make, and there is no escape from the alternative—God or mammon, Jehovah or Baal, heaven or the world.

> Herein is love, not that we loved God, but that he loved us, and sent his Son *to be* the propitiation for our sins. (1 John 4:10)

There is no higher manifestation of love that can exist than the love of God. It is not realized in any love of man to God, but it is realized in God's love to us, that the real nature of love can be perceived.

Such a propitiation reveals a love altogether unique. Herein is love, a love that exists nowhere else. Any love in comparison is only a type or shadow and fades away. It is a love that originated with God the Father and is sustained by him. The bestowment of the greatest possible gift of love, was the atonement of his only begotten Son Jesus, who reconciled us to the Father by his own blood. "Greater love has no one than this, than to lay down one's life for his friends" (John 15:13). He loved us sinners, traitors, alienated ones, the whole world—That we might live, and all who believe might be made heirs of His glory.

Because we have accepted him as our Lord and Savior, his divine love is manifested through our lives to others. This is a love that supersedes our natural love—John says, "We know that we have passed from death to life, because we love the brethren. He who does not love *his* brother abides in death" (I John 3:14). Paul exhorts us in Ephesians with the words, "be imitators of God as dear children. And walk in love, as Christ also has loved us and given Himself for us, an offering and a sacrifice to God for a sweet-smelling aroma" (5:1-2). Because we are begotten of God we should seek to resemble Him. Also, as partakers of the divine nature, we are called to imitate Him; this will be the only way our Savior's supreme manifestation will produce the appropriate effect in us....... Amen!

FOUR

The Power of Criticism

*The trouble with most of us is that we rather be
ruined by praise than saved by criticism*
NORMAN VINCENT PEALE

*Although He was a Son, He learned [active, special]
obedience through what He suffered And, [His com-
pleted experience] making Him perfectly [equipped],
He became the Author and Source of eternal salvation
to all those who give heed and obey Him.*
HEBREWS 5:8-9 (AMP)

The human delusion seems to be the following: we think someone else is always the problem, but not *me*. We tend to export our hate and evil elsewhere. This problem is so central to human nature and human history that its overcoming is at the heart of all spiritual teachings. When we are willing to walk as mature Christians, we find that we are on a short leash and our own feet are always kept to the fire, even as it was with Nathan the prophet approaching David in his sin with Bathsheba the wife of Uriah the

Hittite. "Nathan said to David, 'You *are* the man! Thus says the LORD God of Israel: "I anointed you king over Israel, and I delivered you from the hand of Saul."'...So David said to Nathan, 'I have sinned against the LORD.' And Nathan said to David, 'The LORD also has put away your sin; you shall not die'" (2 Sam. 12:7, 12:13).

The words of the prophet were a decisive test of the character of David. Had he treated the messenger and his message as others have done, David's partial blindness to his sin would have become total blindness, and he would have fallen to a still lower depth, perhaps never to rise again. But his genuine humility enabled him to experience the exceeding grace of God, bringing him to a result that ensured the continuance of his kingdom.

Compare David's response to others, such as "when King Jeroboam heard the saying of the man of God, who cried out against the altar in Bethel, [King Jeroboam] stretched out his hand from the altar, saying, 'Arrest him!' Then his hand, which he stretched out toward him, withered, so that he could not pull it back to himself" (1 Kings 13:4). This really was an indictment against the king's attempt to avenge himself, because he was not willing to receive the message from the prophet.

Also notice King Ahab's disposition being over Israel as he allied with King Jehoshaphat of Judah, telling him "*there is* still one man, Micaiah the son of Imlah, by whom we may inquire of the LORD; but I hate him, because he does not prophesy good concerning me, but evil. And Jehoshaphat said, 'Let not the king say such things!'" (1 Kings 22:8) Ahab's prejudice against Micaiah was based on the fact that he did not like the Word of the Lord that was spoken through him. Ahab did not consider his own wickedness as the issue, but like many people today, reject truth from God because it doesn't agree with their agenda.

As Apostle Paul dealt with Felix the governor of Judah, he reasoned with him "about righteousness, self-control, and the judgment to come, Felix was afraid and answered, 'Go away for now; when I have a convenient time I will call for you'" (Acts 24:25).

Jesus said you shall know the truth, and the truth shall make you free (John 8:32). Jesus also said "this gospel of the kingdom will be preached in all the world as a witness to all the nations, and then the end will come" (Mat. 24:14). No one will be without truth, whether we accept it or reject it we will know the truth.

To know and own truth we must buy it and not sell it, also get wisdom and instruction and understanding, according to Solomon (Prov. 23:23). Buying implies cost, authentication, honesty, and a willingness to pay the price. When you pay the price you now can say I own it because I worked hard for it. The writer of the book of Hebrews tells us "the gospel was preached to us as well as to [Israel in the wilderness]; but the word which they heard did not profit them, not being mixed with faith in those who heard *it*" (4:2).

Jesus said, "whoever hears these sayings of Mine, and does them, I will liken him to a wise man who built his house on the rock: and the rain descended, the floods came, and the winds blew and beat on that house; and it did not fall, for it was founded on the rock. But everyone who hears these sayings of Mine, and does not do them, will be like a foolish man who built his house on the sand: and the rain descended, the floods came, and the winds blew and beat on that house; and it fell. And great was its fall" (Mat. 7:24-27).

People who have not consummated their relationship

with the Lord, or attained a degree of maturity, want one thing and one thing only: control—and they want it now. Pride never wants to change or surrender. The primary message of John the Baptist as he prepared the way for Jesus was "Repent, for the kingdom of heaven is at hand" (Mat. 3:2).

The proclamation at the very center of Jesus's message was "Repent," "change your mind," for the kingdom of heaven is at hand (Mat 4:17). When we consign the word "repent" to deliverance from so-call hot sins only, as opposed to including any actual transformation of consciousness, we miss the mark, which is exactly what sin is. It is true that many Christians are really more concerned about how they appear in the eyes of man. In other words, they are more conscious of the sins man can see than the sins God sees, which is all sin. Jesus said "Woe to you, scribes and Pharisees, hypocrites! For you cleanse the outside of the cup and dish, but inside they are full of extortion and self-indulgence" (Mat. 23:25). Hebrews tells us, "there is no creature hidden from His sight, but all things *are* naked and open to the eyes of Him to whom we *must give* account" (4:13).

The genius of the biblical text is that it has the capacity for course correction and self-critique, actually contained in the book itself! This is necessary and good criticism. Where there is no ability to self-critic, you end up with toxic religion. Thereby ending up with people that cannot tolerate evaluation or criticism and always thinks criticism is coming from enemies.

It seems even to this day, rather than generating its own criticism from within, Christianity has most often been criticized from the outside, by its enemies, who often do not know Christianity's inner values. Most of us have experienced this. Look back in Scripture regarding Saul in Acts 9, breathing out threats and murder against the disciples of the Lord. An outsider as it were, judging from his own understanding, not knowing the New Wineskin that was created called the Church. But, "as he journeyed he came near Damascus, and suddenly a light shone around him from heaven. Then he fell to the ground, and heard a voice saying to him, 'Saul, Saul, why are you persecuting me?' And he said, 'Who are You, Lord?' Then the Lord said, 'I am Jesus, whom you are persecuting. It *is* hard for you to kick against the goads'" (Acts 9:3-5). Until a person has a real encounter with the Lord, their truth will not change. It is only when a person encounters He who is the way, the truth and the life—only then will transformation take place.

Jesus was called a Beelzebub which is also known as the lord of the flies and the prince of the devils. The Pharisees (the religious folk, the church) accused Jesus of using Beelzebub's power to cast out devils (Mat.10:25-26, 12:2). Your good is sometimes labeled evil by folks. As Jesus suffered these accusations he waxed strong, keeping his awareness on his purpose which was Calvary's cross. If Jesus who is perfect was called evil, certainly his followers can expect at least some of the same accusation directed at them. Jesus warns his followers that they will be hated by all for his name's sake. But he who endures to the end will be saved (10:22). As we remain obedient in the face of adversity we will be victorious.

Read the newspapers today, watch the news, listen to the various conversations even among believers; you will see the pattern has not changed. Hating, fearing, or diminishing someone else seems to holds us together for some reason. The creating of necessary victims seems to be in our DNA. Rene Girard calls it "the scapegoat mechanism," which is the central pattern for the creation and maintenance of cultures worldwide since the beginning. The sequence goes something like this: we compare, we copy, we compete, we conflict, we conspire, we condemn, and we crucify. What is important here is that we are able to recognize some variation of this pattern within ourselves, and nip it in the bud, because it will increase as does all sin. Apostle James says, "when desire has conceived, it gives birth to sin; and sin, when it is full-grown, brings forth death" (1:15).

The Scapegoat Ceremony— The Day of Atonement

Aaron shall lay both his hands on the head of the live goat, confess over it all the iniquities of the children of Israel, and all their transgressions, concerning all their sins, putting them on the head of the goat, and shall send *it* away into the wilderness by the hand of a suitable man. The goat shall bear on itself all their iniquities to an uninhabited land; and he shall release the goat in the wilderness (Lev.16:21-22).

The Day of Atonement was the greatest day of the year for Israel. The Hebrew word for "atone" means "to cover." Old Testament sacrifices could not actually remove sins, only cover them. On this day, the people confessed their sins as a nation, and the High Priest went into the Most Holy Place to make atonement for them. Sacrifices were made and blood was shed so that the people's sins could be "covered" until Christ's sacrifice on the cross would give all people the opportunity to have sin removed from their lives forever.

We see here an abbreviated account of the scapegoat ritual. On the Day of the Atonement, a goat was brought into the sanctuary. The High Priest would lay his hands on the goat and all the sins and failures of the people were ceremonially laid on the goat, and the goat was sent out into the desert to die. It was a classic displacement ceremony.

If you really believed that every bad thing you ever did was on a goat and forgotten forever, you'd be beating that goat into the desert too! What immediately follows from the scapegoat story of Leviticus 16 is what is called "The Law of Holiness (Lev. 17-27), which largely defines holiness as separation from evil—which is exactly what they had just performed.

Three thousand years later human consciousness hasn't moved a great deal beyond that, despite the message of the cross. Jesus does not define holiness as separation from evil as much as absorption and transformation of it, wherein I pay the price instead of always asking others to pay the price. This is to say I am responsible for my shortcomings in Christ. As I confess and repent and allow the Savior to transform me to the next level then my success or failure is my responsibility and not someone else's. Paul writes to the Galatians, "let each one examine his own work, and then he will have rejoicing in himself alone, and not in another. For each one shall bear his own load" (6:4-5). This is what moves history from the persistent place of redemptive violence to the divine plan of redemptive suffering.

As it seems today there are not many Christians who have gotten the point. Yet the Scriptures are exceedingly clear. Apostle Peter states, "since Christ suffered for us in the flesh, arm yourselves also with the same mind, for he who has suffered in the flesh has ceased from sin, that he no longer should live the rest of *his* time in the flesh for the lusts of men, but for the will of God" (1 Pet. 4:1-2).

Also, examine Apostle Paul being stoned at Lystra, and later returning to Lystra, Iconium, and Antioch, "strengthening the souls of the disciples, exhorting *them* to continue in the faith, and *saying*, 'We must through many tribulations enter the kingdom of God'" (Acts 14:22).

Paul was stoned because the Jews did not like what he had to say concerning the Gospel of Jesus Christ. There was no willingness to receive the Word of God because it was against their current thinking and tradition. There was no willingness to change or as Jesus said "repent," so that they could experience a new relationship in Him. This is what Jesus related to Nicodemus, "'unless one is born again, he cannot see the kingdom of God.' Nicodemus said to Him, 'How can a man be born when he is old? Can he enter a second time into his mother's womb and be born?' Jesus answered, 'Most assuredly, I say to you, unless one is born of water and the Spirit, he cannot enter the kingdom of God'" (John 3:3-5).

When criticism is allowed and encouraged from within, that criticism is subject to examination of the church. This is what Moses, Jesus, and the apostles did from within the text and in their lifetimes, and why they are true reformers.

Internally generated criticism is the only genuine path of renewal and reform, which even our three-pronged American form of government recognizes. When the church makes room for its own prophets, it is always healthy, which is why Paul called prophecy the second most important gift (1 Cor. 12:28). When it "kills its prophets and stones those who are sent" (Mat. 23:37), it is always in a state of decline—a state of fear instead of faith.

The Corporate Spirit of Religion

The corporate spirit of religion targets its most decisive work on the minds of leaders, individually and collectively.

Its goal is to preserve the status quo of the old wineskin, not allowing the wineskin to move into God's new times and seasons. This spirit works the same today as it did when it caused the Pharisees to equate the traditions of the elders with the sovereign will of God. They asked Jesus, "why do your disciples transgress the traditions of the elders?" (Mat. 15:2) In response, Jesus used harsh language, accusing them of teaching as doctrines the commandments of men (Mat. 15:9). Jesus also said, "you have made the commandment of God of no effect by your tradition" (Mat. 15:6). The Pharisees clearly were not able to advance because they were not willing to hear what the Spirit had to say to usher in this new kingdom.

In this passage of Scripture we see Jesus's implication of the progressive movement of the Spirit as He was questioned by the Pharisees concerning John's disciples. He spoke a parable to them, saying that "no one puts a piece from a new garment on an old one; otherwise the new makes a tear, and also the piece that was *taken* out of the new does not match the old. And no one puts new wine into old wineskins; or else the new wine will burst the wineskins and be spilled, and the wineskins will be ruined. But new wine must be put into new wineskins, and both are preserved. And no one, having drunk old *wine,* immediately desires new; for he says, 'the old is better'" (Luke 5:36-39).

Bottles were goatskins sewed together at the edges to form watertight bags. New wine expands as it ages, so it had to be put in new, pliable wineskins. A used skin, more rigid, would burst and spill the wine. Like old wineskins, the Pharisees were too rigid to accept Jesus, who could not be contained in their traditions or rules. Christianity required new approaches, new traditions and structures. So our church programs and ministries should not be so structured that they have no room for the New Thing of the Spirit of God. "Behold, I will do a new thing, now it shall spring forth; shall you not know it? I will even make a road in the wilderness *and* rivers in the desert" (Isa. 43:19).

Of course this will require a new method and new ideas that will take you from your comfort zone into new horizons as you are willing to be obedient. We can't allow our hearts to become so rigid that they prevent us from accepting the new way of thinking that Christ brings. We need to keep our hearts pliable so we can accept Jesus's life-changing message. I really sense in this hour our Lord wants to release a new anointing upon his saints, like we have never experienced before. In this hour the church is preparing for the double portion as it has been for a long time. Many are tired of the ordinary, mundane, predictable, dull, humdrum, boring, approach to serving the Lord. The Lord has heard the cries of the remnant calling for the latter rain, rain of the Spirit that causes the church to operate in the real power of God and demonstration of the Holy Ghost!!!

Keep Your Map in Christ Current

Millions of Americans and Chinese were shocked when NATO mistakenly bombed the Chinese Embassy on May 7, 1999, during their air raids on Yugoslavia. Apparently, the devastating mistake occurred because the CIA was working off old maps. A political cartoon in the *National Catholic Reporter* showed a flying ace in goggles manning a biplane, trying to read a huge, ancient map entitled "The Ottoman Empire." The letters NATO were proudly emblazoned on the side of the plane.

A once-in-a-lifetime mistake, perhaps? But tell that to the families of the skiers in Italy whose lives were cut short when a low-flying American jet sliced the cable on their ski lift, causing scores of people to tumble to their deaths. The military brass tried to blame the incident on a "hot-dogging" pilot, yet their prosecution plan fell apart when the defense showed that the maps provided to the pilot and crew showed no ski slopes, ski resort, or ski lifts on them. The military's response: "The pilots should have known."

We know for a fact ourselves what is true today on a map does not mean it's true tomorrow. Jesus came as a change agent to make more perfect all the maps before Him. Essentially, what he was saying was "The way to God is not through killing sheep and pigeons or by works—it is through me." God doesn't want burnt sacrifices, He want us to "…. present our bodies a living sacrifice, holy, acceptable to God, *which is* your reasonable service. And do not be conformed to this world, but be transformed by the renewing of your mind, that you may prove what *is* that good and acceptable and perfect will of God." (Romans 12:1-2)

Redemptive Suffering

There are three clear scapegoats in Scripture: John the Baptist, Jesus, and Stephen. Yet John the Baptist's words are very different than Stephen's words before he dies. The reason is because of Jesus's ministry, his death and resurrection, happening between John the Baptist and Stephen. Concerning John the Baptist, he knew by Divine necessity that Jesus must increase, and he, John, must decrease (John 3:30). It is much the same with us as minister of the Lord. No matter the strength of our gifting and anointing; the glory belongs to the Lord. Our assignment is self-depletion as we prepare the way of the Lord in human hearts. Ours is to expand the Kingdom of God and fade off the scene as all the ministers of Christ have done before us. The New Testament ministers hid themselves behind the greater glory, while in today's climate many are self-promoting and auditioning before God and his people as opposed to speaking the truth in love. Apostle Paul says in his second letter to the Corinthians:

> For we do not preach ourselves, but Christ Jesus the Lord, and ourselves your bondservants for Jesus's sake. For it is the God who commanded light to shine out of darkness, who has shone in our hearts to *give* the light of the knowledge of the glory of God in the face of Jesus Christ. (4:5-6)

Jesus said, "I say to you, among those born of women there is not a greater prophet than John the Baptist; but he who is least in the kingdom of God is greater than he." (Luke 7:28) The last clause of the verse is, that, as great as John was, still, he that is least among Christians who have been born of God and have accepted as an article of their faith the crucifixion and ascension of the Son of God, is greater than that great prophet; or, in other words, the humblest child of the new kingdom is superior to the greatest prophet of the old.

By the time you get to the death of Stephen in Act 7, Stephen accepts his death and forgives his enemies. Even the Sanhedrin said that "his face shone like the face of an angel" (Acts 6:15).

Stephen spoke to the problem strongly as he preaches throughout the chapter. Yet he apparently faces his persecution

and death with joy. Stephen was not combative or opposi-
tional, or hateful, but said as he was being stoned, "'Lord Jesus,
receive my spirit.' Then he knelt down and cried out with a
loud voice, 'Lord, do not charge them with this sin.' And when
he had said this, he fell asleep" (Acts 7:59-60).

Stephen is called by some the "proto-martyr" of Christianity, and has become a new Jesus, which is the only and
never-ending goal of every believer even as we are being
conformed to his image. For more we need look no farther
than Hebrews to know the martyrdom of these first century
Christians who died in the faith: "who through faith sub-
dued kingdoms, worked righteousness, obtained promises,
stopped the mouths of lions, quenched the violence of fire,
escaped the edge of the sword, out of weakness were made
strong, became valiant in battle, turned to fight the armies of
the aliens." (11:33-34)

Jesus and Stephen stated the truth, then forgave, then
they were killed. Jesus rose from the dead as the "first fruit"
of those who died in the faith. Paul said, "now Christ is risen
from the dead, *and* has become the first fruits of those who
have fallen asleep" (1 Cor. 15:20).

The image of Jesus as the "lamb of God" first mentioned
by the Baptist (John 1:36) takes on a heroic meaning that is
central to history. The Lamb, which is certainly not a natural
or logical God image, is enthroned at the center and judgment seat of all things (Rev.5:6-8:1). The Lamb is presented
as the one who opens "the seven seals," as if he were the
code to understanding history; he stands perpetually slain
(Rev. 5:6, 5:12) and perpetually victorious (7:10) at the same
time. Both sides of this paradox are presented as inseparable.
There is no life without death, there is no death without life.
It is called, "the Passover mystery."

Some have called this part of Revelation "The Lamb's War," which is a totally different way of dealing with evil. Absorbing it in God, which is the real meaning of the suffering body of Jesus, instead of attacking it from the outside.

I conclude this chapter with this. The New Testament passion accounts go out of their way to point out that it was precisely the high priests, elders, and leaders of the people, Caiaphas, Herod, and Pilate, both church and state, who judged Jesus to be the problem. Every authority in sight is trotted out to judge him unworthy. Then, to add insult to injury, they release a clearly violent man like Barabbas (Mat. 27:26).

The world desires violent partners as opposed to nonviolent ones because it gives them a clear target and a credible enemy. The world is actually relieved to have terrorists to shoot at, and Barabbases loose on the streets. The powers that be are aware that nonviolent prophets are a much deeper problem. They are a much deeper problem because they refuse to buy into the very illusions that the whole world is built on, which is redemptive violence—"They will put you out of the synagogues; yes, the time is coming that whoever kills you will think that he offers God service" (John 16:2). ......Amen!

FIVE

Our Identity in Christ

*You have no idea what a poor opinion I have
of myself—and how little I deserve it.*
W. S. GILBERT

*Know, first, who you are, and then
adorn yourself accordingly.*
EPICTETUS

*God said, "Let Us [Father, Son, and Holy Spirit] make
mankind in Our image, after Our likeness, and let them
have complete authority over the fish of the sea, the birds
of the air, the [tame] beasts, and over all of the earth, and
over everything that creeps upon the earth." So God created man in His own image, in the image and likeness of
God He created him; male and female He created them.*
GENESIS 1:26-27 (AMP)

It is most important that we see ourselves in a right per-
spective in this life because it helps create the foundation
for our relationship with God and man. The Apostle Paul
reminds us in Romans that, "through the grace given to me,

to everyone who is among you, not to think *of himself* more highly than he ought to think, but to think soberly, as God has dealt to each one a measure of faith" (12:3).

Healthy self-esteem is important because some of us think too little of ourselves; on the other hand, some of us overestimate ourselves. The key to an honest and accurate evaluation is knowing the basis of our self-worth, our new identity in Christ. Apart from Him, we aren't capable of very much by eternal standards; in Him, we are valuable and capable of worthy service. Evaluating yourself by the worldly standards of success and achievement can cause you to think too much about your worth in the eyes of others and miss your true value in God's eyes.

I believe one of the greatest problems we deal with today in our churches is unworthiness. Many feel they lack merit, which I believe is the main reason for just a small fraction of most congregations doing the work of the ministry. Unworthiness is the deep-seated belief that tells us we're undeserving, not good enough, inadequate, or just fundamentally deficient.

It's the essential fundamental doubt we feel in the pit of our stomach when we consider living a dream. "Don't try it," unworthiness warns. "Don't even think about it." And so, we don't even think about it. Our mind goes off on one distraction after another; anything rather than having to face even the possibility of our own inadequacy. Of all the components of the comfort zone, unworthiness is the most hideous, and therefore, the most hidden, especially from ourselves.

Physically, unworthiness resides in the area of the solar plexus, an area just below the breastbone where the ribcage forms an inverted "V." In some Eastern traditions, they call this the center of chi, a fundamental point for focusing energy and moving ahead in life. Unworthiness inhibits that energy.

Abraham Lincoln pointed out, "It is difficult to make a man miserable while he feels he is worthy of himself and claims kindred to the great God who made him."

Paraphrasing Lincoln in the negative (which is what unworthiness always does): "It is easy to make a man miserable while he feels he is unworthy of himself and not good enough to claim kindred to the great God who made him."

This is why we must realize that the most important relationship in life one will have, is the one you have with yourself. If you have that, any other relationship is a plus and not a must. Identity, knowing your worth and value is what gives you self-confidence—purpose in life and affinity with other people. We live in a day when it is harder to develop identity because we are living in a very dynamic world. The manifestation of not being comfortable with yourself is to try to bring others down so one can feel good about his or her self. Many have not been validated by their parents or their significant other. Some think they are what they do rather than who they are. Like King Saul who was "image conscious, always wanting to please people;" because of this deficiency he lost favor with God. So it is with all who suffer from an identity crisis, trying to please the people rather than God.

It is important to know that the first notion of value, eternity and image, is planted by God within us at our creation. "Then God said, 'Let Us make man in our image, according to our likeness'...Then God blessed them, and God said to them, 'Be fruitful and multiply; fill the earth and subdue it; have dominion over the fish of the sea, over the birds of the air, and over every living thing that moves on the earth'" (Gen. 1:26, 1:28).

This speaks to the fact that our beginning was very good, just as God wanted it to be. It was the precise relationship that God wanted between Himself and man, so that man could fulfill his ordained purpose in the earth. The Psalmist said it perfectly well when he ask the question; "where can I go from Your Spirit? Or where can I flee from your presence?" (139:7).

It is because we are so much a part of God that there is no way we can escape the presence of the Lord. Even the Greek scholars on Mars Hill had some knowledge of this, as Apostle Paul addressed them in Chapter 17 of Acts, stating: "He has made from one blood every nation of men to dwell on all the face of the earth, and has determined their pre-appointed times and the boundaries of their dwellings, so that they should seek the Lord, in the hope that they might grope for Him and find Him, though He is not far from each one of us; **for in Him we live and move and have our being,** as also some of your own poets have said, 'For we are also His offspring'" (26-28).

This should give us excellent clarity in knowing our identity, and the "who" or, the "self" we are working with. The great illusion that we must all overcome is the illusion of separateness from God. It is almost the only task of religion; to communicate, not worthiness, but union with God, to reconnect people to their original identity. The Bible revelation is about awakening, not accomplishing, realization, not a performance principle; you can't get there, you can only be there. Paul says, God is not far from each one of us (Acts 17:27).

Paul also points out, "*the word is near you, in your mouth and in your heart*' (that is, the word of faith which we preach): that if you confess with your mouth the Lord Jesus and believe in your heart that God has raised Him from the dead, you will be saved. For with the heart one believes unto righteousness, and with the mouth confession is made unto salvation. For the Scripture says, *'Whoever believes on Him will not be put to shame'"* (Rom.10:8-11).

Believing that Jesus is risen from the dead, and that the resurrection is an essential Christian belief; we must believe that not only Jesus lived, but also that he lives. We must not only know about Christ; we must know him. He is not just a historical personage, however great; he is living with a real presence. It is not only knowing Christ the martyr: he is the victor too.

It is not only believing in your heart; but confession must be made with the mouth. It is belief plus confession; it involves witness before men. Not only God but our fellow men must know what side we are on.

Purpose

Dr. Myles Munroe, who was the founder and president of Bahamas Faith Ministries International, wrote extensively on the "Pursuit of Purpose." He writes, "the greatest tragedy in life is not death; it is life without purpose. The most important discovery in life is the discovery of purpose." Purpose is defined as the original intent or motivation of a thing. Simply put, purpose is the "why" of a thing. Without a clear understanding of purpose life becomes an experiment. Where purpose is not known abuse is inevitable. Purpose protects us from doing something good at the expense of doing something right.

King Solomon says, "There are many plans in a man's heart, nevertheless the LORD'S counsel—that will stand" (Prov.19:21).

This Scripture implies the priority of purpose as compared to a man's plan of action. It suggest that the most important interest of the Creator is His original intent for His actions and creation. Many Christians are aimless and without purpose as they strive to serve God. I've had countless people stand at the altar confessing they have come seeking their purpose in Christ. For some that come to the altar it is given to me as a leader to share with them their particular calling or purpose, others it is not. Yet it is for every born-again believer to know their function in the Kingdom of God.

For this to take place in every believer, the process is found in the Epistle of James 4:4-10—"Adulterers and adulteresses! Do you not know that friendship with the world is enmity with God? Whoever therefore wants to be a friend of the world makes himself an enemy of God. Or do you think that the Scripture says in vain, 'The Spirit who dwells in us yearns jealously?' But He gives more grace. Therefore He says: *'God resists the proud, But gives grace to the humble.'* Therefore submit to God. Resist the devil and he will flee from you. Draw near to God and He will draw near to you. Cleanse *your* hands, *you* sinners; and purify *your* hearts, *you* double-minded. Lament and mourn and weep! Let your laughter be turned to mourning and *your* joy to gloom. Humble yourselves in the sight of the Lord, and He will lift you up."

Apostle Peter seems to agree, saying, "Likewise you younger people, submit yourselves to *your* elders. Yes, all of *you* be submissive to one another, and be clothed with humility, for *'God resists the proud, But gives grace to the humble.'* Therefore humble yourselves under the mighty hand of God, that He may exalt you in due time, casting all your care upon Him, for He cares for you. Be sober, be vigilant; because your adversary the devil walks about like a roaring lion, seeking whom he may devour. Resist him, steadfast in the faith, knowing that the same sufferings are experienced by your brotherhood in the world" (1 Pet. 5:5-9).

There is clearly a connection between what Apostle Peter says, and what Apostle James says. In Apostle Peter the quotation is followed by the injunction, "Humble yourselves therefore under the mighty hand of God....Your adversary the devil, as a roaring lion walks about, seeking whom he may devour: whom withstand in the faith." While Apostle James proceeds, "Be subject therefore unto God; but resist the devil, and he will flee from you."

The Apostle James notes there is an antagonism between the love of the world and the love of God. "You adulteresses," is the keynote of the chord which he strikes in his appeal. God is the rightful Spiritual Husband of every professing Christian; and so, if such a one embraces the world, he or she resembles a woman who turns away from her lawful husband to follow other lovers. This represents the condition of the heart. As such it is the description of the spirit and guiding disposition of the unbeliever's life, which is the will to "be a friend of the world." Since accordingly, this friendship represents direct opposition to the Divine will, every man who seeks it first and most, declares himself by that very act "an enemy of God."

The worldly disposition, which shows itself in covetousness and envy and strife, is opposed both to the letter and the spirit of God. And the moral teaching of God's Word on this subject is not "in vain." The Bible means what it says. There is a consciousness of the renewed heart. "Does the Spirit (Holy Spirit) which he made to dwell in us long unto envying or jealousy?" We know well that the power of the Holy Ghost within, as we yield to Him will produce very different fruit from that of envy and strife as we can see in Galatians 5:19-23, representing the works of the flesh and the fruit of the Spirit.

It is only the pure in heart who can see God, and therefore, only as we draw nigh to Him, and by God drawing nigh to us, can we maintain this purity of heart. And He who has placed purpose in us will bring it forth by the excellence of His power. The Apostle Paul declares: "we have this treasure in earthen vessels; that the excellence of the power may be of God and not of us" (2 Cor. 4:7).

It takes humility to know and fulfill your determined purpose. Where there is pride there is delusion, illusion, deception, and self-deception that a person lives in. In that person's innermost being he is bound to be double-minded. Therefore the Apostle James says: purify your hearts, you double minded. In other words, let your hearts be girded in truth—purpose only one thing, (the will of God) for therein is the heart's purity.

And again it is of this same purity of heart that the Apostle James is speaking when he says: "If any of you lacks wisdom, let him ask of God, who gives to all liberally and without reproach, and it will be given to him. But let him ask in faith, with no doubting, for he who doubts is like a wave of the sea driven and tossed by the wind. For let not that man suppose that he will receive anything from the Lord; *he is* a double-minded man, unstable in all his ways" (1:5-8).

The true path to knowing your purpose is going behind the veil, or as Jesus said: "When you pray, go into your room, and when you have shut your door, pray to your Father who *is* in the secret *place;* and your Father who sees in secret will reward you openly" (Mat. 6:6). Only then will you know for yourself.

One Talent People
MATTHEW 25:14-30 / LUKE 19:11-27

Then he who had received the one talent came and said, "Lord, I knew you to be a hard man, reaping where you have not sown, and gathering where you have not scattered seed. And I was afraid, and went and hid your talent in the ground. Look, *there* you have *what is* yours." But his lord answered and said to him, "You wicked and lazy servant, you knew that I reap where I have not sown, and gather where I have not scattered seed. So you ought to have deposited my money with the bankers, and at my coming I would have received back my own with interest. Therefore take the talent from him, and give *it* to him who has ten talents. For to everyone who has, more will be given, and he will have abundance; but from him who does not have, even what he has will be taken away. And cast the unprofitable servant into the outer darkness. There will be weeping and gnashing of teeth." (Mat. 25:24-30)

Then another came, saying, "Master, here is your mina, which I have kept put away in a handkerchief. For I feared you, because you are an austere man. You collect what you did not deposit, and reap what you did not sow." And he said to him, "Out of your own mouth I will judge you, *you* wicked servant. You knew that I was an austere man, collecting what I did not deposit and reaping what I did not sow. Why then did you not put my money in the bank, that at my coming I might have collected it with interest? 'And he said to those who stood by, 'Take the mina from him, and give

it to him who has ten minas." (But they said to him,
"Master, he has ten minas.") "For I say to you, that to
everyone who has will be given; and from him who does
not have, even what he has will be taken away from
him. But bring here those enemies of mine, who did not
want me to reign over them, and slay *them* before me."
(Luke 19:20-27).

The central theme of both parables is the same. Each concerns a man of wealth and authority who commits a certain
sum to each of his servants to administer on his behalf and
then takes a journey to a distant country. After a considerable lapse of time, this wealthy man returns and holds an
individual reckoning with his servants as to the way in which
each has handled the money committed to him.

In both parables three servants are mentioned individually: the first two are faithful in administering their master's money; the third is unfaithful. This is how the money
was distributed in the parable of the talents: "and to one he
gave five talents, to another two, and to another one, to each
according to his own ability" (Matt. 25:15). A talent was a
considerable quantity of money, perhaps as much as fifteen
years' wages.

Notice that this verse reveals the principle according to
which the talents are distributed: "to each according to his
own ability." That is, God distributes to each believer the
maximum number of talents that his own ability will permit
him to use effectively. God does not give to any believer
either more or less than he is able to use effectively.

In this parable the first two servants each achieved an
increase of one hundred percent. The servant who had
received five talents gained five more; the Lord assessed the

faithfulness of these servants not by their net gain but by their percentage increase. The servant who gained five talents was not considered more faithful than the servant who had gained two talents, although his net gain in talents was greater. Rather, each of these servants achieved proportionate increase: one hundred percent.

This is indicated by the fact that the words of commendation spoken to these two servants, recorded in Mat. 25:21-23, are exactly the same in each verse. "His lord said to him, 'Well *done,* good and faithful servant; you were faithful over a few things, I will make you ruler over many things. Enter into the joy of your lord.' He also who had received two talents came and said, 'Lord, you delivered to me two talents; look, I have gained two more talents besides them.' His lord said to him, 'Well *done,* good and faithful servant; you have been faithful over a few things, I will make you ruler over many things. Enter into the joy of your lord.'"

Each of them originally received the maximum number of talents that his ability would allow him to use effectively; each of them had achieved the maximum gain possible—one hundred percent. It is on their faithfulness, as expressed in the percentage increase achieved, that their judgment is based. The fact that one man originally received five talents and the other two is not the basis on which their faithfulness is assessed.

In this parable of the talents the third servant merely hid the one talent he had received and later brought it back to his lord in exactly the same condition in which he had received it. For this he was not only deprived of a reward, but he was also totally and finally rejected and cast out from his lord's presence.

There can be no doubt whatever about the meaning of these words. This third servant not only received no reward; he was actually deprived of the one talent which he had originally received, and he himself was cast out from his lord's presence.

Now turn to the parable of the minas in Luke 19. A mina was a quantity of money equivalent to about three months' wages.

In this parable ten servants are mentioned, although only the cases of three of them are described in detail. Originally, all ten servants received the same amount committed to them by their lord: one mina each. Of the three servants whose cases are described, the first gained ten minas, the second gained five minas, and the third merely hid his mina away and eventually brought it back in the condition in which he had received it.

It would appear that each of these three servants possessed equal ability, since each received the same amount committed to him. However, they were not equally faithful. The first gained twice as much with his mina as the second. For this reason his reward was twice as great.

"Then came the first, saying, 'Master, your mina has earned ten minas.' And he said to him, 'Well *done,* good servant; because you were faithful in a very little, have authority over ten cities.' And the second came, saying, 'Master, your mina has earned five minas.' Likewise he said to him, 'You also be over five cities'" (Luke 19:16-19).

We notice that, in two respects, the reward of the first servant was greater than that of the second. The first servant was specifically commended by his lord as a good servant; the second servant received no such special commendation. Second, the first servant was given authority over ten cities; the second servant was given authority only over five cities. That is to say, their rewards were in exact proportion to the increase which each had achieved.

One further conclusion we may draw from this parable is that rewards for serving Christ faithfully in this present age will consist in positions of authority and responsibility in the administration of Christ's kingdom in the following age. In other words, faithful service in the present age leads to continued and extended opportunities of service in the next age. For those who truly love Christ there can be no greater joy or privilege than that of continuing to serve their Lord. For those who are faithful, this privilege, begun here in time, will be extended throughout the ages of eternity.

In this parable of the minas, as in that of the talents, the third servant was condemned for being unfaithful and failing to make any use at all of the mina committed to him. In this parable, as in that of the talents, the unfaithful servant not only received no reward, but even the one mina he had originally received was taken away from him. The final end of the servant with the one mina is not revealed in this parable. However, it seems reasonable to conclude that, like the unfaithful servant in the parable of the talents, he was rejected and cast out from his lord's presence.

In both parables alike, failure to make active use of the talent or mina committed to each servant is described by the very strong word "wicked." In each case the lord commences his judgment of the unfaithful servant by the phrase "you wicked servant." We learn also, that, by God's standards, wickedness consists not only in actively doing that which is bad, but just as much in the failure to do good when it lies within our power to do it.

Jesus is coming back, we know this is true. Yet, there are those who are of the opinion what they are given to work with by our Lord in his kingdom does not amount to much in comparison to the gifts and talents of others. As a result many will not use what they have, and are striving for what the Lord has given others. We must realize that we are held responsible for what the Lord has purposed in us, and concentrate on that, and not on what others are accomplishing. We must stand before the Lord for ourselves.

Also, there can be no doubt that originally in this parable the whole attention is riveted on the useless servant. There can be little doubt that he stands for the Scribes and the Pharisees, and for their attitude to the Law and the truth of God. The useless servant buried his talent in the ground, in order that he might hand it back to his master exactly as it was. The whole aim of the Scribes and Pharisees was to keep the law exactly as it was. In their own phrase, they sought "to build a fence around the Law." Any change, any development, any alteration, anything new was to them anathema. Their method involved the paralysis of religious truth.

Lord help me to advance, adapt, pursue, persevere, press toward the high calling in Christ Jesus our Lord, with and through all you have given me!!! Amen!

SIX

The School of Love

Love is an act of endless forgiveness
PETER USTINOV

*IF I [can] speak in the tongues of men and [even] of
angels, but have not love (that reasoning, intentional,
spiritual devotion such as is inspired by God's love for
and in us), I am only a noisy gong or a clanging cymbal.
And if I have prophetic powers (the gift of interpreting
the divine will and purpose), and understand all the
secret truths and mysteries and possess all knowledge,
and if I have [sufficient] faith so that I can remove
mountains, but have not love (God's love in me)
I am nothing (a useless nobody).*
1 CORINTHIANS 13:1-2 (AMP)

In Genesis 7 we find the famous story of Noah and the flood. It is probably a story in Scripture that piques more curiosity than any other story in the Bible. Questions like: How did Noah get all those animals in the ark? How did he feed all of them the forty days and nights of the flood? And the major question: Who did the cleaning? This is why this story is so loved by children and adults. God tells Noah to bring into the ark all the opposites: the wild and the domestic, the crawling and the flying, the clean and the unclean, the male and the female of each animal (Genesis 7:2-15).

In itself, that is understandable. But then God does a most amazing thing. God locks them together inside the ark (Genesis 7:16).

When we make note of the fact that God closed them in— that God puts all the natural animosities, all the opposites together, and holds them together in one place it speaks to more than just the preservation of the species. Some would say that it speaks to our ability to balance all the opposites within us. Especially when you realize you are a mixed blessing, and that you are filled with contradictions, and that you are a mystery even to yourself. When one is able to accept that fact, then you won't pretend that you can totally eliminate all that you consider unworthy from yourself. As Jesus said in the Parable of the Weeds and the Wheat, "don't pull out the weeds, or you might pull out the wheat along with it, let them both grow together until the harvest, and at that time I'll do the separating" (Matthew 13:29-30).

It is also a picture of the Kingdom of Heaven. Jesus said, "The kingdom of heaven is like a net cast into the sea and gathered of every kind" (Matthew 13:47). The church being the physical manifestation of the kingdom of heaven; as the wheat and the weeds must remain together until the day of separation, so it must be in our churches. In John 17 Jesus prayed to his Father that his followers would not be taken out of the world, but kept from the evil in the world (17:15). Our faith must eventually be revealed in our love for one another beyond those who are the same as us.

In this we actually learn how to live "holding" things unreconciled—leaving them partly unresolved and without perfect closure or explanation. This teaches us how to live in hope. There is a process of growth and maturity taking place as John says, "It does not yet appear what we shall be, but we know when He appears, we shall be like Him. And every one that has this hope in Him purifies himself even as He is pure." (1 John 3:2-3) The ego always wants to settle the dust quickly and have answers now. But Paul says, "In hope we are saved yet hope is not hope if its object is seen" (Romans 8:24).

The ark therefore is an image of how God liberates and refines us. The ark is an image of the People of God (the church) if you will on the waves of time, carrying the contradictions, the opposites, the tensions and the paradoxes of humanity.

You'd think we would claw one another to death inside, which we have done from time to time. But that gathering of contraries is, in fact, the school of salvation, and the school of love. That's where it happens, in honest community and committed relationships. Love is learned in the encounter with the "otherness" says Martin Buber and Emmanuel Levinas, who were both Jewish philosophers whose worldview was formed by the Bible.

Eventually we give this mutual humble submission and respect a word: forgiveness. We sometimes think that shaking a fist (threateningly, with all the remembered transgressions) is the way to get something. A shaking fist tends to beget a shaking (or swinging) fist. To receive, forgive. To get, forget.

Henry Ward Beecher wrote: "I can forgive, but I cannot forget," is only another way of saying, "I will not forgive."

Forgiveness ought to be like a cancelled note—torn in two, and burned up. So that it never can be shown against one.

Remembering a grievance locks you into remembering hurt, pain, anger, betrayal, and disappointment. Who on earth wants that? Let it go. Forgive it away.

Forgive the past. Then forget it. Let it go. It is not worth remembering. None of it is worth remembering. What's worth experiencing is the joy of this moment.

Apostle Paul says, "You should bare one another's burdens, and so fulfill the law of Christ" (Galatians 6:2). Forgiveness becomes central to Jesus's teaching, because to receive reality is always to "bear it," to bear reality for not meeting all, if any, of our needs. To accept reality is to forgive reality for being what it is.

Probably forgiveness is the only event in which you simultaneously experience three great graces: God's unmerited goodness, the deeper goodness of the one you have forgiven, and then you experience your own gratuitous goodness too. That's the payoff. This makes the mystery of forgiveness an incomparable tool of salvation. There is really nothing else quite like it for inner transformation.

Faith's Role

In this hour, as we are on the seas of time in preparation for eternity we must immerse ourselves in faith. Even as we are told "to fight the good fight of faith; lay hold on eternal life, whereunto thou art also called, and has professed a good profession before many witnesses" (1 Timothy 6:12). We are called to remain true to God even in the face of opposition, oppression, and adversity. This means to have an unswerving allegiance to the cause of Christ amid hostilities, both internal (the church) and external (the world). Faith causes us to enter salvation but we grow through understanding and obedience. We must grow up to be built up. We can't grow starting over at every crisis

God wants us to be resolute concerning the things of Him. Many have their relationship with God based on circumstances—if things are going our way or not. But we are reminded by Apostle James "that the trying of your faith works patience" (1:3). In this adversity we must take advantage of the invitation we are given; that is to ask God in faith for wisdom so our desires can be aligned with the Lord's purposes. Not only that, but you must asked in faith not doubting, or wavering, if we waver you are like a wave of the sea driven with the wind and tossed (1:4-6). A mind that wavers is not completely convinced that God's way is best. It treats God's Word like any human advice retaining the option of disobedience. It vacillates between feelings, the world's ideas, and God's commands. If your faith is new, weak, or struggling, remember God is trustworthy, be loyal to Him. To stabilize your wavering or doubtful mind, commit yourself wholeheartedly to God.

It is faith that brings all the benefits of salvation into our lives, all of His exceedingly great and precious promises. The Lord, "has given us all things that pertain unto life and godliness, through the knowledge of Him who has called us to glory and virtue" (2 Peter 1:3-4).

So we can see the biblical tradition, and Jesus in particular, both praise faith even more often than love. Because faith is that patience with mystery that allows you to negotiate the stages. As Gerald May points out in his book, *Dark night of the Soul*, it allows God to lead you through the darkness where God knows and I don't. This is the only way to come to love. Love is the true goal, but faith is the process of getting there, and hope is the willingness to live without resolution or closure. "Which hope we have as an anchor of our soul, both sure and steadfast" (Heb. 6:19). No matter what storms we face and no matter how rough the waves of adversity crash against us, we stand firm upon his exceedingly great and precious promises because he will complete the work he has begun in us.

Jonah's Imposition

Jonah doesn't want to go and preach to the Ninevites because, like a member of any group, he does not like his God caring about other people! Does this sound familiar? Possessed with this national hatred of idolatrous Gentiles, and fearing that God, in his great long-suffering, might, after all, spare these Assyrians to whom he was sent, he attempted to escape the assignment. He knew his duty, but at the present moment he was determined to avoid its fulfilment. Accordingly, he fled to Joppa and took ship for Tarshish. The providence of God followed him. A violent storm arose, and the mariners of the vessel, surmising that it was sent by God began both to pray and to throw precious cargo overboard attempting to ease the ship of its burden, or to ease them of their troubles (Jonah 1:5).

There is even today a lot of precious things being sacrificed needlessly that has nothing to do with the cause of the storms of this life. When it comes to us as individuals, engaged in storm after storm seemingly not able to find solace in life, obedience to the Word of God and the voice of the Lord is the answer. As far as the Church is concerned—She is called to "Awake!" I heard the voice of the Lord as I was in prayer saying, "Awake!"

> Awake, awake; put on the strength, O Zion; put on thy beautiful garments..... (Isaiah 52:1).

> And that, knowing the time, that now it is high time to awake out of sleep: for now is our salvation nearer than when we believed. The night is far spent, the day is at hand let us therefore cast off the works of darkness, and let us put on the armor of light. (Romans 13:11-12)

> If my people, which are called by my name, shall humble themselves, and pray, and seek my face, and turn from their wicked ways; then will I hear from heaven, and will forgive their sin, and will heal their land. (2 Chron. 7:14)

The mariners cast lots in order to discover who the guilty person was among them. Jonah, being chosen, confesses the truth, and at his own earnest request is cast into the sea. Jonah is, however, not drowned. A huge fish swallows him, and after three days vomits him forth, and he lands safely on the shore. He then humbly obeys the will of God, sets out, and executes his mission to Nineveh. The king of that city, having heard probably of his strange deliverance from the deep, and believing him to be a messenger from Heaven, ordered a general fast, and by timely repentance averted the threatened doom.

This really speaks to the truth that the church and the world are locked together on the same boat. We as a people representing the Kingdom of God miss the mark when we point the finger at the world as the chief cause of the storms that rage, throwing the world into chaos. When the church (the people of God) are disobedient to God's purpose chaos is created. Much of the problems the world face today can be remedied if the church would come into alignment with its calling. Jonah knew he was the cause of the storm. He simply did not like the people God was telling him to preach to. As I said in the earlier chapters, the way you relate to one another is the way you relate to God. "If a man say, 'I love God,' and hate his brother, he is a liar: for he that love not his brother whom he hath seen, how can he love God whom he hath not seen?" (1 John 4:20). And again: "For God so loved the world, that he gave his only begotten Son, that whosoever believeth in him should not perish, but have everlasting life" (John 3:16).

So God says to Jonah in the last verse of the book, "Am I not free to feel sorry for Nineveh?" (4:11).

What God was doing, was laying the foundation for a universal compassion, and not just a small superiority system, which is what Jonah, the unwilling prophet, seemed to want. Jonah's rebellion even placed the heathen sailors in the category of possible believers: their cry to the Lord, fear of the Lord, and the fact that they offered sacrifice and made vows to him. So, in this view, the history is levelled against the bigotry and exclusiveness of the Jews which come forward so prominently in later times. God has compassion on all men, "In every nation he that fear him, and work righteousness, is accepted with him" (Acts 10:35).

This story of Jonah speaks to every minister's conviction as it relates to the assignment being God's assignment, or their own. We must move from doing my work for God, to letting God do God's work in and through me. Again, the prophet

Isaiah reminds us, "'For my thoughts are not your thought, neither are your ways my ways,' saith the Lord. 'For as the heavens are higher than the earth, so are my ways higher than your ways, and my thoughts than your thoughts'" (55:8-9).

Today's Confusion

As we all know, human history is in a time of great flux, of great cultural and spiritual change. The mind doesn't know what to do with so much information. We are told that if you take all of the information that human beings had up until 1900, and call that one unit, that unit now has doubled every ten years. That's the confusion and anxiety that we're dealing with today, especially in our children and in people who are not grounded.

In light of today's information overload, people are looking for a few clear certitudes by which to define themselves. Satisfying untruth, or lies, seems to be more pleasing to us than unsatisfying truth, and full truth is invariably unsatisfying. We live in a day it seems so many people are not interested in the truth. They are only interested in their point of view, or as some might call it, the "alternative truth."

Transformed people, on the other hand, are always seeking a balance between opposites, a very subtle but creative balance. As William Johnston, S.J., once said, "Faith is that breakthrough into that deep realm of the soul which accepts paradox with humility." When you go to one side or the other too much, you find yourself either overly righteous or overly skeptical and cynical. There must be a healthy middle and I hope that is what we are looking for here, as we try to hold both the needed light and the necessary darkness.

Take for example the contrast between liberals and conservatives. On the one hand conservatives are biblical but not contemporary, while on the other the liberals and radicals are contemporary but not biblical. Why must we polarize in this naïve way? Each side has a legitimate concern, the one to conserve God's revelation, the other to relate meaningfully to real people, in the real world. Why can we not combine each other's concerns? Is it not possible for liberals to learn from conservatives the necessity of conserving the fundamentals of historic, biblical Christianity and for conservatives to learn from liberals the necessity of relating these radically and relevantly to the real world?

Meanwhile, each group stays on its favorite side of the cultural chasm, and almost nobody seems to be building bridges. Yet we preachers are supposed to be in the business of communication. There is a need to relate God's unchanging Word to our ever-changing world— refusing to sacrifice truth to relevance or relevance to truth; but resolve instead in equal measure to be faithful to Scripture and pertinent to today.

If we are conservatives (I am referring to our theology, not our temperament or our politics), and stand in the tradition of historic Christian orthodoxy, we live on the Bible side of the gulf. That is where we feel comfortable and safe. We believe the Bible, love the Bible, read the Bible, study the Bible and expound the Bible.

So why would the church preach the gospel of politics in favor of either side of the political spectrum as if God is representative of one side or the other? This is the chief avenue to gender contention and strife and division, it hinders the Love of God and Unity of the Spirit in the Body of Christ. The Apostolic Prophetic Church must stand in the Spiritual authority it has been given by God. It is the perfect means to display God's manifold or multifaceted wisdom to rulers and authorities in heavenly realms. The keys to the Kingdom are in the hands of the church to bind and to lose.

Consider Micaiah who King Ahab hated, because he prophesied truth, and to King Jehoshaphat of Judah who were preparing for Battle against the Syrians. "He said, 'I saw all Israel scattered upon the hills, as sheep that have not a shepherd'" (1 Kings 22:17). Nathan was a court prophet who lived in the time of King David. Later, he came to David to reprimand him for committing adultery with Bathsheba while she was the wife of Uriah the Hittite, whose death the king had also arranged to hide his previous transgression (2 Samuel 12:7-14). Paul's talk with Felix the governor became so personal that Felix felt convicted, like Herod Antipas (Mark 6:17-18), had taken another man's wife. Paul's words were interesting until they focused on righteousness, temperance, and judgment to come. Trembling, Felix ask Paul to go away and come at a more convenient time (Acts 24:24-25). Not to mention King Agrippa who when Paul gave his testimony said "you almost persuaded me to be a Christian" (Acts 26:28).

When the church becomes akin or related to a political party, and prophesies in favor of what that party represents as if it is the supreme authority, the church then becomes an instrument of a system alien to God. In Jeremiah 23:32, God speaks through the prophet Jeremiah saying, "'Behold, I am against them that prophesy false dreams,' says the Lord, 'and do tell them, and case my people to err by their lies, and by their lightness; yet I sent them not, nor commanded them; therefore they shall not profit this people at all,' says the Lord."

The church in general has fallen into the category of backing and promoting one running for president and if that person is elected of course magnifies their success and minimizes their faults and failures. Because of a stance to back a particular party, the church, the prophet, God's ambassador has compromised his mission in favor of an ideology as opposed to the Gospel of Jesus Christ, and has lost their ability to speak the truth to power.

There is a great portion of the church that has embraced Donald J. Trump as the forty-fifth president to the United States. His surprise upset over Hillary Clinton had a tremendous impact on the nation for what seems to me very obvious reasons, primarily relating to his character and bombastic personality. Yet it is apparent why he was so embraced by the religious community amidst all the prophetic signs and analogies from his name, his age, the timing of his presidency, etc. with the Bible.

This, in spite of the fact that one of the major issues of President Trump's claim to fame was the perpetuation of the "Birther Lie." This lie became an entire conspiracy theory movement against the first Black president of the United States, President Barack Obama. The more Mr. Trump repeated it the more famous he became. Thus his ascendency to the office of president. As a result his objective was to undo every piece of legislation President Obama put in place, majorly the Affordable Care Act, but to no avail. Trump's entire four years as president were surrounded by intrigue and controversy beginning with Robert Mueller's *Report on the Investigation into Russian Interference in the 2016 Election.* The impeachment of Donald Trump was initiated on December 18, 2019 when the House of Representatives approved articles of impeachment on charges of abuse of power and obstruction of Congress. The Senate acquitted Trump of these charges on February 5, 2020. The documentation resulting from Mueller's report handed down numerous indictments and prison sentences to those in Trump's cabinet and associates. It's noted that Donald J. Trump has had the most corrupt administration in American history as he now scrambles to issue pardons to family members and others in his administration under investigation.

My question is: why is the church so obsessed with the Republican Party and Donald J. Trump in particular, whose agenda is so clearly Antichrist in his actions? This is the main reason why the prophet's role is to stand outside of the fray of the political arena. The church will always be embarrassed when she embraces a particular political party, no matter what side she align herself with.

President Trump now leaves office with his claim to fame as the only president in United States history to have been impeached twice. Now, on the charge of insurrection on the day that Vice President Mike Pence, presiding over the joint session, announced the tally of electoral votes certifying Joe Biden's win. This violent insurrection left five people dead as the Capitol Building was stormed by a mob equipped to take it over and capture Vice President Pence along with Speaker of the House Nancy Pelosi.

Not since the dark days of the Civil War and its aftermath has Washington, D.C. seen a day quite like Wednesday, January 6, 2021 when the Capitol Building was stormed by violent insurrectionists leaving five dead in its aftermath.

President Trump's term is climaxing in an outbreak of violence and recrimination at a time when the country has fractured deeply, and without doubt has lost a sense of itself as leaders of other nations look on in despair toward the United

States, the beacon of democracy. Notions of truth and reality have been splintered. Faith in the system has eroded. Anger is the one common ground.

Joe Biden is now president, with an outgoing President Donald Trump leaving office in disgrace. Never really admitting he lost the election fairly. Also failing in his many attempts to overturn the election of his opponent, who has clearly won by over seven million votes. The reality surrounding how he emerged as president is equal to that of his demise as he runs around the country in denial of his loss, attempting to do what I in my lifetime have never seen happen.

Barack Obama on the other hand, if we are truthful, was a man of poise, dignity, empathy and grace. Even dealing with the systemic racism in this country which many deny exist. The famous vow of Mitch McConnell "to block Obama's agenda and to make him a one-term president." For eight years we may fault him on some of his policies, but never on his character. His family held the dignity and respect of the office of president and the White House. He was a president for all the people, including gay rights which he is much maligned for by the church. I maintain the opinion that it is the mission of the church to bring people to Christ. It is the job of the President to provide legislation for the good and welfare of all the people—the good the bad and the ugly.

It is the church that is being weighed in the balances and found wanting in this hour of pandemic. The church must stop walking in lockstep with a particular party of our government. It has caused those who are not grounded in Christ to follow man and not Christ. We know these are the last days because as Jesus stated, "We must be careful not to be deceived, also, the love of many has waxed cold." It is hard to find commonality in the Body of Christ because the church has made it so you must be on one side of the political chasm or the other. It seems as though "unity" means "sameness" as opposed to having the ability to come together as a result of the Cross of Jesus Christ.

Our Perception of Jesus

In Matthew 11:20-24, Jesus began to denounce the cities in which most of his miracles had been performed because they did not repent. When John came to the end of his gospel, he wrote a sentence in which he indicated how impossible it was ever to write a complete account of the life of Jesus: "But there are also many other things which Jesus did; were every one of them to be written, I suppose that the world itself could not contain the books that would be written" (John 21:25). This passage of Matthew is one of the proofs of that saying.

It is clear the most tremendous things of Jesus's ministry happened in these towns, and yet we have no account of them whatsoever. There is no record in the gospels of the work that Jesus did, and of the wonders he performed in these places, and yet they must have been amongst his greatest. A passage like this shows us how little we know of Jesus; it shows us—and we must always remember it—that in the gospels we have only the barest selection of Jesus's works. The things we do not know about Jesus far outnumber the things we do know.

Jesus said, "Woe to you Chorazin! Woe to you Bethsaida!" The Greek word for "woe" expresses sorrowful pity at least as much as it does anger. It is the accent of sorrow, the accent of one who offered men the most precious thing in the world and saw it disregarded. Jesus condemnation of sin is holy anger, but the anger comes not from outraged pride, but from a broken heart.

The sin of Chorazin, of Bethsaida, of Capernaum, was worse than the sin of Tyre and Sidon. And of Sodom and Gomorrah. It must have been very serious for again and again Tyre and Sidon are denounced for their wickedness (Isaiah 23; Jeremiah 25:22, 47:4; Ezekiel 26:3-7, 28:12-22), and Sodom and Gomorrah were and are a byword for iniquity.

It was the sin of the people who failed to perceive or forgot the responsibilities of privilege. To the cities of Galilee had been given a privilege which had never come to Tyre and Sidon, or to Sodom and Gomorrah, for the cities of Galilee had actually seen and heard Jesus. We cannot condemn a man who never had the chance to know any better; but if a man who has had every chance to know the right does the wrong, then he does stand condemned. We do not condemn a child for that for which we would condemn an adult; we would not condemn a savage for conduct which we would condemn in a civilized man; we do not expect the person brought up in the handicaps of a city slum to live the life of a person brought up in a good and comfortable home. The greater our privileges have been, the greater is our condemnation if we fail to shoulder the responsibilities and accept the obligations which these privileges bring with them.

Luke writes: "And that servant, which knew his lord's will, and prepared not himself, neither did according to his will, shall be beaten with many stripes" (12:47).

It was the sin of indifference. These cities did not attack Jesus Christ; they did not drive him from their gates; they did not seek to crucify him; they simply disregarded him.

Neglect can kill as much as persecution can. I am afraid this condition represents many who point the finger of judgment and condemnation today.

Even as I am writing this book—it is sent out for review; some reviewers may praise it, others may damn it; it does not matter so long as it is noticed; the one thing which will kill a book stone dead is if it is never noticed at all for either praise or blame.

And so we are face to face with one great threatening truth: it is also a sin to do nothing. There are sins of action, sins of deed, but there is also a sin of inaction, and of absence of deeds. The sin of Chorazin, of Bethsaida, and of Capernaum was the sin of doing nothing. Many a man's defense is: "But I never did anything." That defense may be in fact his condemnation.

For God himself out of love for the people He has made in His own image, addresses us as human beings. He respects the mind and will He has given us; He refuses to coerce us, and instead asks for our thoughtful, loving and free response. Is this not the reason why the biblical writers encourage their reader to develop critical listening? Elihu was right to say that the ear tests words as the palate tastes food, namely with a view either to savoring it or to spitting it out. As with food, so with ideas, Elihu continues, "let us choose what is right; let us determine among ourselves what is good" (Job 34:1-4). Similarly in the New Testament, Christians were told to test the spirits to see whether they are of God. "Test everything, for only then could they hold fast what is good, and abstain from every form of evil" (1 John 4:1; 1 Thess. 5:19-22). That is, even messages claiming to be inspired had to be evaluated in the light of apostolic teaching. Otherwise, how could the Christian grow and become mature except by having their faculties trained by practice to distinguish good from evil? (Phil.:9-10 / Hebrews 5:14).

Yet, "The thing that hath been, it is that which shall be; and that which is done is that which shall be done: and there is no new thing under the sun. Is there anything whereof it may be said, 'See, this is new?' It hath been already of old time, which was before us" (Eccl. 1:9-10).

Many things remain and will remain in human life. Labor, sorrow, care, struggle, death; love, pleasure, success, honor. When it comes to the typical human characters, we still have with us the false, the licentious, the cruel, the servile, the ambitious, etc.; and we still have the meek, the grateful, the generous, the pure in heart, and the devout. Men will still ask: Whence came we? By whose power are we sustained? To whom are we responsible? Whither do we go? How can we know and serve and please God? Yet the truth of Jesus Christ is: Heaven and earth may pass away, but his words "will not pass away." They are with us still, and they will remain, amid all wreckage, to enlighten our ignorance, to cheer our sorrow, to accompany our loneliness, to conquer our sin, to light up our departure, to bless and to enrich us, ourselves, with the blessings and the treasures that are not of earth but of heaven. Amen!

SCRIPTURE INDEX

—

Chapter One

Revelations 1:5-6

Ephesians 5:27

Matthew 3:2

Matthew 4:17

Matthew 10:7

Luke 1:3

Matthew 24:14

Psalms 145:10-12

1 Corinthians 4:20

Romans 14:17

Hebrews 12:28-29

Matthew 1:21

Matthew 16:16/20

Romans 10:9-13

Luke 17:20-21

Matthew 16:18-19

Colossians 1:12-14

Matthew 6:10

1 Corinthians 12:18

Acts 2:41/47

Acts 5:12-14

Ephesians 4:11-16

Chapter Two

1 Corinthians 1:26-29

Acts 4:13

Jeremiah 9:23-24

Isaiah 45:9

Isaiah 64:8

Jeremiah 18:1-4

Romans 9:20-21

Isaiah 49:1-3

Ephesians 1:4-5

Ephesians 6:17

Hebrews 4:12

Psalms 91:1-2

James 1:2-4

Galatians 4:4-5

Luke 4:18-20

Matthew 4:13-16

Matthew 9:1

2 Corinthians 3:6

John 16:12-15

Psalms 91:14-16

John 15:4-5

Jeremiah 1:5

Psalms 139:16

Isaiah 49:1

2 Peter 1:12-15

1 Corinthians 14:1-3

Chapter Three

Exodus 20:2-5	Deuteronomy 14:1-2	Matthew 22:36-40
2 Corinthians 3:18	2 Kings 18:33-36	Matthew 6:24
Exekiel 18:2-4/27-28	Genesis 1:26	James 4:4
Joshua &:22-25	John 15:14-16	Galatians 1:10-12
Hebrews 11:6	Ephesians 1:3-4	
Exodus 33:18-20	1 John 2:15-17	

Chapter Four

Hebrews 5:8-9	James 1:15	2 Corinthians 4:5-6
2 Samuel 12:7	Leviticus 16:21-22	Luke 7:28
2 Samuel 12:13	Leviticus 16:17-27	Acts 6:15
1 Kings 13:4	Galatians 6:4-5	Acts 7:59-60
1 Kings 22:8	1 Peter 4:1-2	Hebrews 11:33-34
Acts 24:25	Acts 14:21-22	1 Corinthians 15:20
Matthew 3:1-2	John 33:3-5	John 1:36
Matthew 4:17	1 Corinthians 12:28	Revelations 5:6
Matthew 23:25	Matthew 23:37	Revelations 8:1
Hebrews 4:13	Matthew 15:2/6/9	Revelations 5:6/12
Acts 9:1-5	Luke 5:36-39	Matthew 27:26
Matthew 10:25-26	Isaiah 43:19	John 16:2
Matthew 12:24	Romans 12:1-2	
Matthew 10:22	John 3:30	

Chapter Five

John 3:2	Proverbs 19:21	James 1:5-8
Genesis 1:26-28	James 4:4-10	Matthew 6:6
Psalms 139:7	1 Peter 5:5-9	Matthew 25:14-30
Acts 17:26-28	Galatians 5:19-23	Luke 19:11-27
Romans 10:8-11	2 Corinthians 4:7	

Chapter Six

1 Corinthians 13:2	Isaiah 52:1	Matthew 11:20-24
Genesis 7:2-16	Romans 13:11-12	John 21:25
Matthew 13:29-30	2 Chron. 7:14	Luke 12:47
Matthew 13:47	1 John 4:20	Job 34:1-4
John 17:15	Jonah 4:11	1 John 4:1
1 John 3:2-3	Acts 10:35	1 Thess. 5:19-22
Galatians 6:2	Isaiah 55:-9	Phil. 1:9-10
1 Timothy 6:12	1 kings 22:8-17	Hebrews 5:14
James 1:6	2 Samuel 12:7-14	Eccl. 1:9-10
2 Peter 1:2-4	Mark 6:17-18	
Hebrews 6:19	Acts 24:24-25	
Jonah 1:5	Jeremiah 23:32	

RESOURCES

Caussade, Jean-Pierre de. – Abandonment to Divine Providence – Library of Congress – 1751 –Copyright 1975 by John Beevers.

Damazio, Frank – The Making of a Leader – Bible Temple Publishing Portland, OR 97213 – Copyright 1988

Jones, Laurie Beth – Jesus Inc. – Published by Crown Business, New York, New York, Random House, Inc. New York, Toronto, London, Sydney, Auckland.

Nee, Watchman – A Table in the Wilderness – Christian Literature Crusade Fort Washington, Pennsylvania 19034 – Copyright Angus I. Kinnear 1957 – This printing 2000

Rohr, Richard – Things Hidden, Scripture as Spirituality – Published by St. Anthony Messenger Press, Cincinnati, OH. 45202 – Copyright 2008, by Richard Rohr and John Feister.

Wagner, Peter C. – Changing Church – Published by Regal Books From Gospel Light Ventura California, U.S.A. – 2004 C. Peter Wagner.

Peter McWilliams – Do It! Let's Get off Our Buts – Published by Prelude Press 8159 Santa Monica Boulevard, Los Angeles, California 90046 – Copyright 1991–1994

George G. Hunter III – Church for the Unchurched – Copyright 1996 by Abingdon Press Nashville, TN. 37202-0801

John Scott – Between Two Worlds – Published 1982 by William B. Eerdmans Publishing Company, 255 Jefferson Ave., S.E., Grand Rapids, Michigan 49503 –Copyright 1982 by John Scott.

ABOUT THE AUTHOR

William A. Dockery is a former high school teacher and second generational pastor of Memorial Temple Christian Ministries since 1992, succeeding his father Bishop James A. Dockery.

In 1998, he began the implementation of his vision—the construction of a community center in his father's honor. Hence, the completion of the James A. Dockery Community Center, Inc. in September 2000. The James A. Dockery Community Center is a 24,500 square foot building located on the site of Memorial Temple Christian Ministries. Housed within the center is Community Action Organization Head Start, and various community programs.

William has traveled extensively in missions proclaiming the Gospel of Jesus Christ from Moscow, Russia to the Ukraine; the Provinces of Cameroon in West Africa; South Africa; the Dominican Republic; and Juarez, Mexico to mention some areas of travel.

William A. Dockery is a permanent member of Leadership Buffalo and the founder and presiding apostle of Covenant

Ministries International, Inc., which is comprised of a net-
work of churches, para-ministries, and apostolic /prophetic
leaders with a vision of transforming society, by expanding
the Kingdom of God through networking with national and
international multicultural ministries.

*"For [simply] consider your own call,
brethren; not many [of you were considered
to be] wise according to human estimates
and standards, not many influential and powerful,
not many of high and noble birth.
[No] for God selected (deliberately chose)
what in the world is foolish to put the wise to shame,
and what the world calls weak to put the strong
to shame. And God also selected (deliberately chose)
what in the world is lowborn and insignificant
and branded and treated with contempt,
even the things that are nothing, that He might
depose and bring to nothing the things that are,
So that no mortal man should [have pretense for
glorying and] boast in the presence of God."*
1 CORINTHIANS 2:26-29 (AMP)

Made in the USA
Monee, IL
02 July 2021